Questions Jesus Asked

S. V. (Steve) Dedmon

© 2015 S. V. (Steve) Dedmon

All rights reserved. No part of this book shall be reproduced, stored in a retrieval system, or transmitted by any means without the written permission of the author or the publisher.

International Standard Book Number 13: 978-1-60452-109-2
International Standard Book Number 10: 1-60452-109-0
Library of Congress Control Number: 2015960059

BluewaterPress LLC
2922 Bella Flore Ter
New Smyrna Bech FL 32168
Printed in the United States of America

http://bluewaterpress.com

This book may be purchased online by going to -
http://www.bluewaterpress.com and entering the title in the search box.

If your church or organization is interested in bulk purchases of this title, please contact BluewaterPress LLC for bulk ordering discount pricing for Mr. Dedmon's books.

DEDICATION

This is dedicated to my wife, Suzanne,
who continues, besides the Lord Jesus Christ
to be my most ardent advocate and encourager,
and to my daughter, Stefanie, and son Seth
in whom my hope and pride
to see them meet all life's challenges
never wavers nor falters.

PREFACE

This is my second faith-based book. The first, A Layman's Look at the Baptist Faith and Message, was written to give an alliterative overview and outline of the basic tenets of the Southern Baptist faith. Admittedly, I wrote it more as a guide, than to be a narrative. This is written in a narrative style, as I actually write sentences and paragraphs! Drawing more from my experience as a teacher, most, but not all, of the chapters are actual past Bible study lessons I have taught in one form or another.

Early in my spiritual life and growth, I was initially influenced by pastors Dr. Homer Lindsay, Jr. and Dr. Jerry Vines at First Baptist in Jacksonville, Florida and their expository and alliterative preaching and teaching styles as well as later, by Dr. John Phillips. As such, I have embraced it as my personal teaching style. Purposefully, I have written this book in an alliterative manner (notwithstanding the narrative style), which I trust will be easily understood as well as a medium, easily communicated to the reader and the teacher, if used in such a manner. To help with the communication aspects, at the end of each chapter, I have included the outline used throughout the text. Additionally, portions of the text are italicized which correspond to the chapter outlines, thus providing a guide as one is reading through the chapter. In some cases it includes the actual text in the outline, in others, only the concept. As opposed to the first book, I have included personal commentary, examples and contemporary illustrations to be used as the reader or teacher sees fit.

As was the first, this book was written as a product of God laying it on my heart to try to convey what I have not only been taught but learned and applied to my life. In that light, as honestly as possible, I have attempted to be and hopefully have been, biblical, thus spiritually sound. My target audience is the individual learner and those teaching the Word of God. For the individual, my prayer is it will strengthen not only their walk, but also their witness. As to the teacher, my hope is they will have yet another tool to encourage those they teach as they look afresh at the Living Word of God. For both, it is my heart's desire it be spiritually educational as well as spiritually practical to meet those challenges we face as believers in the Lord Jesus Christ.

I would like to Thank Lori Milam for her assistance in the writing of this book. As mentioned previously, some of the chapters are actual Sunday school lessons put to print. Sometimes the spoken word does not translate so well to the written. Lori had the unenviable task of helping with that transition as she read them more in the light of being taught than being a reader. She brought perspective, which was needed and appreciated. Also, my thanks to her husband Pete for his patience in the process.

It is within this backdrop I pray the Lord will be glorified and the individual edified and hopefully enjoy---A Layman's Look at Questions Jesus Asked.

Contents

PREFACE   page xi

INTRODUCTION   page xvii

Chapter 1 . . . . page 1
"Who do men say that I, the Son of man, am?"
Popular Opinion, Matthew 16:13-14

Chapter 2 . . . . page 17
"Why are ye so fearful? How is it that ye have no faith?" Mark 4:35-41

Chapter 3 . . . . page 31
"What wilt thou that I should do unto thee?"
Mark 10:46-52

Chapter 4 . . . . page 45
"Why callest thou me good?" Luke 18:18-30

Chapter 5 . . . . page 61
"What seek ye?" John 1:35-42

Chapter 6 . . . . page 75
"Saul, Saul, why persecutest thou me?"
Acts 9:1-6

Chapter 7 . . . . page 91
"But who say ye that I am?" Personal Opinion, Matthew 16:15-18

ENDNOTES   page 109

Scripture Index   page 113

INTRODUCTION

The primary teaching tool in the box of a law professor is the Socratic Method. Named after the Greek philosopher Socrates, it is based on asking and answering question to enhance one's critical thinking and beliefs related to a specific topic. As related to law school, this method of instruction replaced the lecture method in the mid to late 1800s by professor Christopher Columbus Langdell at Harvard Law School. It then spread to other law schools and has been the nemesis of law school students ever since.

It is one thing to use this teaching method in areas related to the philosophical or the legal, quite another to apply it to the spiritual. What people and society may think about matters related to philosophy or jurisprudence may affect the present and in a lot of instances the future, but the questions Jesus asked and the answers He elicits related to not only their earthly, but their eternity. Questions posed by Socrates may make a person more philosophically enlightened. Those posed by Langdell may make them more legally educated; however, those posed by Jesus dealt with liberty from sin and salvation of the soul. This book looks at those questions and the people whose lives were changed for the better and unfortunately in some cases for the worse.

In Chapter 1 Jesus asks a question related to His identity and thus looks at popular opinion of who people believe He was during His earthly ministry. It explores the people in the old and new testaments Jesus is compared with as related to the characteristics He and they had in common. It then looks at today's society and the popular notions of who, or what, Jesus is.

Chapter 2 looks at fear and faith. Here Jesus deals with His disciples as they encountered a sudden storm. It also looks at the severity and seriousness of that storm as well. All this leads to the question Jesus asks and provides us an analogy between a level of fear as related to the contrasting level of faith. However, even in the question, it shows Jesus' ongoing care and compassion.

Chapter 3 begins much like where Chapter 2 leaves off as it deals with faith. Yet, the circumstances are a bit different as we see a blind man recognizing in Jesus what others failed to see — His Deity and what it could mean to his disability and destiny. Ultimately, it goes further as there is a fickle crowd who is witnessing the whole encounter. Lastly, and this is the key to the question Jesus asks is the issue of the reality of getting the requests we ask from the Lord.

Jesus asks an interesting question in Chapter 4 as it challenges and makes us look at the standards we use to justify our spiritual standing-Good verses

Godly. Here we see a good person yet one who wants to hold fast to his earthly riches as contrasted to heavenly rewards. It also reminds us about the consequences of our earthly desires as related to our heavenly destination.

We go back to the beginning of Jesus' ministry in Chapter 5, as Jesus begins recruiting the team He would use to impact a planet. He asks a question dealing with What the disciples of John were seeking, when in reality He knew it was Who they were seeking that was the crux of the issue. Not only do we see the followers of Jesus in this chapter, but the forerunner of Him as well, as we look at the life of John the Baptist.

Chapter 6 begins in tyranny as Saul's history of persecuting the church is exposed. Here we see persecution of the church, i.e. the body of Christ, is persecution of Christ Himself. We will analogize that persecution with what we endure today as Christians. Eventually we will see from great grief comes great relief. Then finally we will see in our own lives, from the root of tyranny and what appears to be tragedy can come great translation and triumph.

As Chapter 1 began with Popular Opinion of who Jesus is, Chapter 7 ends by Jesus asking the ultimate question one must answer as to what is your Personal Opinion of who He is; one we will answer when face to face with Christ, either on bended or broken knee. Beginning with certain isms, we will conclude with more of the same as Jesus will reveal the source of all spiritual revelation and thus refute the philosophies of this world.

There is an old adage among trial lawyers you may be familiar with-Never ask a question you do not know the answer to. I would like to take that and look at it in a spiritual context. As you read this book, keep this in mind.

For all of life's circumstances, confrontations, challenges or celebrations, *Jesus Never Asks A Question He Is Not The Answer To.*

Questions Jesus Asked

Chapter 1
"Who do men say that I, the Son of man, am?"
Public Opinion
Matthew 16:13-14

Who do men say Jesus really is? Jesus himself thought this important enough to ask those who were closest to Him, this same question. On a daily basis, either politically where someone running for office is asked about their faith, or socially, on a popular talk show, or spiritually when discussing what differentiates one denomination from another or the differences between religions, the question or actually the answer to who men say Jesus really is has become a volatile hot topic issue. Always cognizant of issues, Jesus confronts his disciples with the same question. This quesiton as to Jesus' identity is just as relevant a question today for you and me as it was two thousand years ago.

One arena, where the answer to who men say Jesus is, resides in the court of Public Opinion. Notice the disciples' answer in verse 14 of Matthew 16. Reading the King James Version of the Bible the text uses the term "some say." If you went to a popular mall and took a survey and asked people to give a short answer to the question of who Jesus is you would get the same results the disciples articulated – "some say." I have no doubt the answers would fall into the same categories to those the disciples named.

The first answer the disciples give is that Jesus was John the Baptist, a *great preacher*. John the Baptist was indeed a great preacher. John as we know was the cousin of Jesus as Mary, the mother of Jesus, was the cousin of Elisabeth, John's mother as related in Luke 1:36. Here we also see the unusual circumstances of John's birth. In Luke Chapter 1, we see the *message regarding his birth* in verse 13, the *miracle of his conception* in verses 18 and 24, then his *mission until his death* in verses 16 and 17.

It is also in Luke's gospel where we see John's *expectancy in the presence of the Lord* as ..." the babe (John) leaped in her womb," in verse 41 to be followed later by his *humility in the presence of the Lord* in Matthew 3:14 where John says he needed to be baptized by Jesus. Prior to that, in Matthew 3:11, John was honest and humbled when he said, "but he who cometh after me is mightier than I, whose shoes I am not worthy to bear."

In Luke 3:3-20 we see John preaching on a variety of topics. From repentance for the remission of sins, the need for baptism, challenging the religious establishment of the day, to preparing the way of the Lord, John is a preacher. By the world identifying Jesus as John the Baptist and the disciples acknowledging this, they are also raising an interesting phenomenon of the day.

In Matthew 14:1-12 is the account of Herod's conviction and anguish over the beheading of John the Baptist. Due to the weight of his sin he says to his servants Jesus is John the Baptist, risen from the dead. So, in this regard, Herod is spearheading public opinion regarding who Jesus is as a reincarnation of John the Baptist, the preacher. This should come as no surprise as today some television, movie, rock or social star will proclaim Jesus was only a preacher of some sort and as such attempt to relegate Him to a subservient position other than that of being the Son of God and redeemer of mankind.

Do not misunderstand, Jesus was every bit the preacher as he expounded the same themes as John the Baptist, but he did so not as mortal man but immortal savior of mankind. However, when people, no matter their status or stature proclaim Jesus to be only a preacher, you and I have an obligation to challenge the totality of such a statement. As you have probably witnessed in your own experience, there is no shortage of people who believe Christ to be only a preacher.

In the court of public opinion, the next person Jesus is compared to is Elijah. In 1 Kings 17, we are introduced to him. As you may recall, Elijah had a special ministry. It was special in that he lived during the reign of Ahab, who the Bible says in 1 Kings 16:30 "did evil in the sight of the Lord above all who were before him." The next verse includes additional ungodly indictments as it says he "walked in the sins of Jeroboam and took as his wife Jezebel … and served Baal and worshiped him." Summing up his ungodliness, in verse 33 the Bible says, "Ahab made an idol and Ahab did more to provoke the Lord God of Israel to anger than all the kings of Israel who were before." With that addition to his resume, Ahab now has the dubious distinction of being the worst of a long line of ungodly rulers. How would you like that to be your testimony?

His wife, Jezebel is no spiritual jewel herself. She slays the prophets of the Lord in 1 Kings 18:13. Then as recounted in 1 Kings 21, to get her pouting husband Ahab a vineyard he wanted, she devises a plot which ends in the murder of an innocent man. Thus, you have the times in which Elijah lived. As a quick point, historically, you and I have read about or lived in times of ungodly leaders, whether political, social and in some cases, the most shameful of all — spiritual.

Ungodliness in leadership should neither surprise, nor shock us. God is aware of those who use, misuse, or abuse, their position for personal, financial, or political gain. Our responsibility, as Elijah did, is to stand against wickedness. We did not stand up when those in leadership removed God from the classroom and we wonder why our youth are sexually active and morally insensitive. We bowed and accepted alternative lifestyles and are now having to defend the definition of marriage as being between a man and a woman. We listened as society trumpeted personal freedoms as those who have no voice lose their lives as another means of personal birth control.

In our lifetime, we have seen the highest office in our country disgraced by definitely immoral, and possibly criminal acts. When immorality and ungodliness raises its ugly head, and it will, it should be met with the godly lives and godly lips of godly people - you and me. Elijah had his challenges and we have ours. Those challenges may have different names, but sin has been and will always be sin and we who know Jesus as Lord and Savior should position ourselves to stand against it.

So...in comparison to Jesus, public opinion compares Him to Elijah as a *provider* and a *physician*. 1 Kings 17:12-16 is the account of Elijah asking for food, of a widow from whom God had directed him. She replies truthfully that she only has a handful of meal and a little oil to provide food for herself and her son, which the widow sees as only enough to relieve them of suffering until their death. Elijah reassures her in verse 13 and proclaims in verse 14 the amount, although apparently small, will not only be sufficient for this meal but will continue to meet their needs.

Knowing the scriptures, those in Jesus' day were able to make the same comparison. As you may or may not be aware, on two separate occasions, Jesus took a lunch portion of loaves and fish, and fed four thousand and five thousand people, respectively. The scriptures relate, just as in the 1 Kings account, there was not only enough to meet the demand but there were leftovers.

For us, we need to understand there are only those who only see Jesus as a provider to meet their physical needs. I am not saying He does not indeed do that, however, too many times we want Christ and His provision without making a profession in Him. As to those Jesus feed, I always wonder where they were when Pilate asks whom they would have him release after his trial and in fact were any of them yelling "crucify him" as related in John 19:15. Where were they during his march through the streets of Jerusalem on his way to Golgotha? They were where I am too many times, denying my relationship with Him when I believe He has let me down as provider or has failed me in some other spiritual or practical way.

Elijah was also a physician. 1 Kings 17: 17 continues the above account of the widow and her son. At this point in the story the son dies. Elijah consoles the widow, lays his body on the son and the miraculous happens, the boy, once dead is now alive. Although Jesus healed people with infirmities on numerous occasions, my focus is on three He raised from the dead. Mark 5:22-43 deals with a young girl, the daughter of Jairus. In Matthew 8:6 Jesus heals the servant of the Roman centurion, and of course, there is Lazarus, probably the most recognized.

In each of these accounts, Jesus hopes to focus on three distinct characteristics of God. First, we see *His commitment.* In the account of the young girl, Jesus says to all the onlookers, "the child is not dead, she sleepeth" (Mark 5:39). Their response is to laugh Him to scorn (v. 40). The commitment aspect is shown in that this young girl was the daughter of a ruler of the synagogue. Jesus came to the nation of Israel, God's chosen people and this is an instance of His commitment to the present Jewish generation and the generation represented by the life of the young girl.

Jesus never lost sight of wanting to see His Father's chosen people redeemed spiritually and rescued politically, a commitment that will ultimately come to fruition when Jesus returns as detailed in The Revelation. Throughout the scriptures, Jesus lovingly and longingly pleads for Israel to return to God and to restore them to fellowship with the Father. Although my commitment may waiver or falter, Jesus remains committed to me, presently in life and ultimately will do so in death.

In Luke 7:11-18 we see the account of a widow whose son was dead. Interestingly, we are not given the name of either the widow or the son although we are given the name of the city-Nain. This is the only time the city is named in the New Testament but it illustrates how Jesus went where He was needed, and got there exactly on time. Pertaining to our Lord's timing, someone once said Jesus made haste but was never in a hurry. Here the scripture specifically says, "when the Lord saw her, he had compassion on her and said unto her, Weep not" (Luke 7:13).

Jesus understood then and understands now, our hurts. He sees through us to the hurt in our hearts as manifested by the tears in our eyes. Note the scripture makes it a point to tell us what He says to the widow, "Weep not" (v. 13). He then goes beyond acknowledging her pain but alleviates it as He tells her dead son to...Arise. As opposed to my actions, and too many times lack thereof, Jesus' *compassion* took Him to unknown places to touch unknown people.

Then there is Lazarus. Jesus now shows His *commiseration*. Here we have a family dynamic of which Jesus had been a part for some time. Jesus had dealt with Lazarus' sister Martha and Mary in Luke 10:40-42. In that account we have an example of administrating activities for Jesus as in the case of Martha, as opposed to absolutely adoring Him as in Mary's case.

In John 11, the circumstances have drastically changed from the peaceful setting in a home to the woeful setting of a funeral. This time all the sisters see is the tragedy of death and its finality. Jesus will show them the triumph in death and a glimmer of His complete authority over it. The death of their brother has the sisters distraught. These circumstances are a bit different as Jesus has a history with Lazarus, Martha and Mary.

One issue is the insinuation by Martha and Mary of blame brought on by the emotions that rise from the death of a loved one. Blame in that they say had Jesus been there, their brother would not have died (John 11:21). Like the sisters, we sometimes forget death is inevitable. Like Martha and Mary, we also want to blame someone or something when we suffer the loss of a loved one. Too often, we forget death is a product of sin. Adam was created for physical immortality, but forfeited that by his disobedience.

Specifically, the Bible addresses this in Genesis 2:18 and 3:19. I realize these verses are preached and taught to reference spiritual death and those are spiritual truths. However, there is nothing to suggest it could not be strictly construed to reference physical death. Man was engineered by God to live physically for an eternity. If we listen to the evolutionist, we should be living longer, if in fact we are evolving. Interesting as well is how those espousing evolution as a science, want to ignore the 2nd law of thermodynamics.

This law suggests entropy (the arrow of time) works in such a manner that things become more disordered as time increases, not more ordered. The Bible acknowledges and confirms the science as our ancestors lived close to a millennium and we can barely make it past a century. Ultimately, unless Jesus returns and I am taken up in the gloriousness of the Rapture, my eternity will be in heaven, but blame for my death is not the issue, as death is inevitable.

Going back to my point, people die and we do everything we can to postpone the unavoidable. So, Mary and Martha blame Jesus. Society is no different. News headlines chronicle death, then society looks for answers or someone to blame and ultimately Jesus is that someone. How many times have you heard, if there was a loving God how could He allow this, that, or the other to happen? Again, asking the right question is always at the core of an issue. How could God not allow it to happen? With man shunning God, why are we surprised at how man's inhumanity to man is exemplified. History is wrought with the shameful manner humanity has attempted to exalt itself on one hand and in so doing eradicate itself on the other.

The point is not God's insensitivity to death, but man's depravity regarding life, whether that life is in either the physical or spiritual. Hebrews 9:27 describes there is a when to death... "It is appointed unto men once to die," and there is a why to death..."but after this the judgment;" however, do you note there is no mention as to how one will die? Thus blame, or the how, is second to the reality of death and what relationship we have with Jesus when faced with that reality.

Continuing with the story regarding Lazarus, when Jesus arrives, it is a very emotional scene and the tears were streaming down the cheeks and sorrow flowing from the heart. The anguish is not lost on Jesus as He deals with the sisters' grief and that of others. Even in the context of having professional mourners, a common practice of the time, passions were flowing. Jesus himself is moved in His spirit as the scripture says he groaned and was troubled (John 11:33). Then in verse 35 there is the shortest verse grammatically speaking in the Bible, but one immeasurable profound spiritually; Jesus wept. Think about the precious tears of Jesus.

The first mention of tears in the Bible is in Genesis when Abraham weeps when his beloved Sarah dies. Tears are the subject of Psalms 56:3 where the psalmist states, then asks, "Put thou my tears in thy bottle. Are they not in thy books?" Characteristically, mourners would catch their tears in water skins and place them at the tomb of their loved one. We even see tears in heaven, as John is overwhelmed in Revelation 5:4.

Can you imagine how treasured would Jesus' tears have been at the tomb of Lazarus? Ever wonder what events through the ages have brought tears to His eyes? Maybe He has shed a tear at the death of His beloved disciples as they refused to disavow their love for Him, or during the premeditated extermination of the Jews in WWII, or when He heard the cries of the living babies as they died before their birth. Or, maybe a tear of joy at the translation of the Holy Scriptures for the common man to read and contemplate whenever their heart so convicted them to do so. Wonder of wonder, the tears of Jesus. The tears were wiped away from the eyes and the joy was returned to the heart, when Lazarus bound in ceremonial burial clothes, either floated or flew from his tomb. At that point, people say yet again, like Elijah, Jesus as a great physician.

Next, in verse 13 of Luke 11 is the Public Opinion that compares Jesus to Jeremiah. In the book that bears his name, we are given the account of his prophecies regarding the fall of Jerusalem and his choice to stay with the Jewish remnant that chose not to go to Babylon under the rule of King Nebuchadnezzar. Like Jeremiah, Jesus proclaimed the fate of the nation if they failed to heed God's warning. As such, public opinion then and now sees Jesus historically, as it saw Jeremiah biblically, as a modern day *prophet*. Jeremiah Chapter 2 is replete with Jeremiah pointing out how Israel had changed their gods (v. 11), forsaken God (v.13) and become but a broken shell of all God had established them to be as a people and how Jeremiah warned them of the consequences of their attitudes and actions. Ultimately, in Chapters 39 and 52 all Jeremiah had prophesied came to fruition as Jerusalem fell, Zedekiah loses his sons, his eyes, and his life dying in prison because of Nebuchadnezzar's invading armies entering the city.

If you remember, Jesus' ministry did the same as He warned the Jewish nation. The scripture address how the multitudes described Jesus in Matthew 21:11 as the prophet of Nazareth of Galilee. He constantly addressed issues raised by the Pharisees and Sadducees-from healing on the Sabbath, eating with sinners, praying in public, the greatest commandment, tithing, and the ultimate rejection of him as Messiah.

In John 19:15, there is an incredible indictment of the Jewish nation and how they had moved so far from God. Here, boldly, openly, and unashamedly, the chief priest declare their allegiance to a pagan king-Caesar. Jesus also speaks and warns the Jews of the fate of Jerusalem in Luke 21:20-24. Historically, as you may be aware,

Titus destroyed Jerusalem, in approximately 70 A.D., affirming the Lord's prophetic words. Expounding on these verses, Jesus speaks prophetically regarding Jerusalem and its destruction in Matthew 24. So...in the realm of public opinion, Jesus' proclamations were not lost on the nation, whether they believed them to be true or not, as they did in Jeremiah's time, they could not help notice the comparisons in Jeremiah's and Jesus' messages as prophets.

Jeremiah was also a *pleader*, in that he pleads to God on behalf of the people and in some cases on his own behalf as well. In Jeremiah 2:2, we see the prophet receiving the word of the Lord coming to Jeremiah telling him to "Go and cry in the hearing of Jerusalem." The word, "hearing" in this translation, means ears. Directly to the ears of the Jews, God through a pleading Jeremiah, sets the tone for the whole book in Jeremiah 2:11-13.

Here the scripture says they have *abandoned God* as he states, "Hath a nation changed their gods, which are yet not gods"? Then in verse 12, their attitude *appalls Heaven* as the scripture says "Be appalled, O ye Heavens at this..." Finally, in verse 13 the Bible reiterates they have abandoned God, as they have "forsaken me, the fountain of living water and adds... and hewed out cisterns, broken cisterns, that can hold no water" thus, they *allow and accept spiritual emptiness*.

Jesus, during his ministry, dealt with these exact issues. Do you recall Pilate's question and the answer of the chief priests in John 19:15, as mentioned above when asked, "Shall I crucify your King"? Abandoning their Messiah and King, as did earlier generations, they say, "We have no king but Caesar." Earlier, in

Luke 19:41-44, when entering Jerusalem we saw an instance of Jesus being emotionally overcome as He plead for His people. Specifically, the Bible said He (Jesus) "beheld the city, and wept over it." Next, heaven must have been amazed and appalled at the events surrounding the birth and death of Jesus.

In Matthew 2:2, we see a star is born announcing Jesus' birth and the means for the wise men to find the babe. However, as glorious as this event is, it was just as appalling the tragedy to follow as Herod orders the extermination of children from two years old and under as recorded in Matthew 2:16. Just as appalling is Christ's death on the cross. In that instance heaven responds as the sun mourns resulting in three hours of darkness over the whole land, as outlined in Mark 15:33. Not only does the sun mourn, but the stones split/speak (Matthew 27:51/Luke 19:40), supluchers release and saints testify (Matthew 27:52-53).

Lastly, there is the Jew's spiritual emptiness Jesus encountered. This is addressed in Luke 13:34-35 as He speaks directly to Jerusalem saying they have killed their prophets and how, notwithstanding Jesus' attempt to gather them back to Him, they refused. Tragically, Jesus then declares in verse 35, "your house is left unto you desolate." It is one thing for the Jews to have disregarded the pleadings of Jeremiah, yet quite another to later hold in distain the pleadings of Jesus. However, we will see people do the same today.

Abandoning God, Appalling Heaven, and Allowing and Accepting Spiritual Emptiness are as pertinent and practical today as they were to Jeremiah and Jesus. To illustrate, I am going to use popular "isms" embraced by today's society that encompass the characteristics of these three spiritual deficiencies. This will not be a comprehensive list as I am going to deal with some more of them in the last chapter, but hopefully you will understand my use of them as related to this section.

The first would be *polytheism*-the belief in multiple gods. Today's society has made gods of fame, money, power, sex, social status and the ones you are adding to list as you read this. Another would be *pantheism*-god is in the forces of the universe. This view sees god in the beauty, power and mystery of the universe. So, whether it is the sun, moon, stars, planets, they all evidence a god.

Related to and expounding on this concept would be *deism*-god created everything but has left it to its natural conclusion. That being the case, god would now expand his existence into all nature. As such, he is in the tree, plant, flower, fog, mist, rain, and essentially everything, but with no involvement with man. Then there is *factualism*-god is only in those things that can be scientifically proved. It is from here science uses the Big Bang Theory to substantiate their factual claims.

Digressing just a little, as to taking this theory at face value, how many big bangs do you imagine would be needed to take acres and acres of Boeing 747 parts, assuming you actually had the correct pieces, to make a commercially viable aircraft? Evolution then becomes a widely held viable working theory ultimately used to oppose scripturally based Creationism and Intelligent Design.

Just as the Jews did in Jeremiah and Jesus' day,

today's society has embraced these "isms" resulting in Abandoning God, Appalling Heaven, and Allowing and Accepting Spiritual Emptiness. These attitudes as well as the people we have looked at show how challenging and diverse the debate is as to Jesus. The disciples were confronted with a very challenging and complex question. They responded with great insight that is as applicable today as it was 2000 years ago. Incredibly, the answers were much the same.

However, as we will see in the last chapter, Public Opinion is only half the issue and ultimately of no consequence when considered in the light of eternity. Yet, "Who do men say I, the Son of man am?" is still a question you and I need to answer to be effective witnesses for Christ.

Chapter Outline

I. John the Baptist – the Preacher
   A. Message regarding his birth
   B. Miracle of his conception
   C. Mission until his death
   D. Expectancy in the Presence of the Lord
   E. Humility in the Presence of the Lord

II. Elijah
   A. Provider
   B. Physician
        1. Jesus'
           a. Commitment
           b. Compassion
           c. Commiseration

III. Jeremiah
   A. Prophet
   B. Pleader
        1. Attitude of the People
           a. Abandoned God
           b. Appalled Heaven
           c. Allow and Accept Spiritual Emptiness
               (1)   Polytheism
               (2)   Pantheism
               (3)   Deism
               (4)   Factualism

Chapter 2
"Why are ye so fearful? How is it that ye have no faith?"
Mark 4:35-41

In the first 34 verses of the fourth Chapter of Mark's gospel we see the Lord teaching. You have most likely heard that a parable is an earthly story with a heavenly meaning. As a previous resident in heaven and a present one on earth, Jesus had the perfect perspective on which to teach spiritual truths based in practical application. In fact, any spiritual teaching without practical application is practically useless. No good is gained by leaving the message from the pulpit in the pew! My personal expectation when hearing God's word is that it will instantly change my life. That may sound unrealistic, but if I do not truly believe God can change lives, then why should I attend church? No matter the method used to communicate the Word to me whether it was by reading, teaching or preaching it should be resonate in my life through my living it; if I have "ears to hear" (Mark 4:9).

An outline of Mark 4 would reveal Jesus teaching parables about *sowing and reaping* in verses 1-12. In verses 13-20 Jesus is *explaining* the previous verses, focusing on the seed being the word and reiterating it's where it is placed, how it is planted, if it is plucked or ultimately polluted, that reveals its ultimate potential. He then moves to a parable on *lighting and hiding* in verses 21-25 as related to *our ways*. From there, the focus is on *walking* in verses 26-29 as Jesus puts the emphasis on our *growing*. Finally, Jesus is *comparing* our faith to that of a mustard seed as He teaches on what will ultimately be our *welcome* in verses 30-34. It is with this backdrop in the beginning of the chapter, the *parables* are spoken to the multitudes. We now find in the end of the chapter, how Jesus speaks to the disciples in the midst of a *problem*.

After a long day with the multitudes, Jesus and the disciples load up the boats and depart for Gerasa. Unbeknownst to them they are about to go from the tranquility of the seaside to the tumult of the sea. Verse 37 says, "there arose a great storm of wind," which affected the sea, as it beats against the boat and causes calamity amongst the disciples.

In Florida, where I live, we understand how quickly storms can arise, particularly in the summer. The sky goes from being blue with a few puffy clouds to being black with clouds looking like those Dorothy and Toto faced in the Wizard of Oz. Sometimes, you can see both sky conditions at the same time depending on which direction you are looking. Within only a few miles you can see the sun brightly shining, lightening brightly flashing, all the while hearing the thunder loudly clapping.

Recently, I experienced those very circumstances. As I was on my way to play tennis, there appeared to be one large lone cloud. On each side, the sky was blue and the sun was shining. Suddenly, I saw a single lightening bolt, but did not think much of it, as it appeared to be associated with a singular building and dissipating summer shower. Literally, one minute later raindrops about the size of a silver dollar began to hit the windshield, yet the car was bathed in sunlight. As I continued to drive, the raindrops got smaller, but more frequent, accompanied by the sound of the drops hitting the roof. By the time I got a half-mile from the first time a drop of rain hit the car, I was now engulfed in not only torrential rain, but dime-sized hail as well.

As the hailstones pummeled the car I begin to look for relief from nature's barrage. Just as I am pulling under a tree to provide some form of shelter, my wife calls me on my cellphone. As we are talking and I tell Suzanne of my plight, she informs me the noise associated with the hailstones hitting the car is so loud she cannot hear me. With the conversation cut short, I look to the south and behind me to the west, and see nothing but sunshine. Looking back, this was one special storm as it combined all the classic elements. Depending on which direction I looked, there was wind, rain, hail and sunshine. If the disciples faced circumstances anywhere related to those I experienced, I can relate to the suddenness of a storm.

Just as what happened to me, the disciples were faced with a storm that developed suddenly and without warning. The storms of life happen the same way. A car pulls out in front of you while driving, resulting in an accident. Something falls off the truck you are following and you have to swerve, which causes a chain reaction accident. Your sister tells you she has been diagnosed with cancer. You get a phone call notifying you that your tumor is not benign. Life's storms come up abruptly, allowing no time to prepare for the emotional, mental, or physical trauma they may bring.

For the disciples, minutes before, their skies were blue as they were listening to Jesus teaching heavenly parables. With a gentle breeze at their back and the water lapping placidly against the bow of the boat, all was well. Yet, like my scenario, there were hints that something was going to change and not necessarily for the best. Then before the disciples knew it, there is a sudden storm and the clouds are black, the winds are boisterous, and waves are beating the boat. Just like the weather, the storms of life *come up suddenly*, in the midst of fleeting blue skies.

Expanding on the examples above, the storms of life are also *severe*. In the case of the disciples, the boat is taking on water. In fact, verse 37 says the boat was now full, or in nautical vernacular it was swamped and sinking. I do not know much about boats, but the water is supposed to be on the outside, not the inside! Life's storms bring the problems from the outside to the inside. Note also, and all too often we gloss over or read the scriptures like it is just another story but there is another issue.

Did you notice in verse 36 its reference to "other little boats?" There is no reason to think they were not facing the same storm and were in trouble as well. The storms of life may directly affect a specific person or group, but they can indirectly affect others as well. When I was laid off from my position as a construction manager from my father's company (more on that in subsequent chapters), it was not just me who could have suffered the possible negative consequences; it was my wife and children as well. Whether those affected are husbands, wives, children, other relatives, or friends, storms have tentacles and reach beyond the obvious. I would contend the more severe the storm the larger the number of participants, but also the audience. People, for varying reasons, want to see how Christians respond to the storms of life either to ridicule them or rejoice with them. So, whether all the boats were in trouble or just the one with Jesus in it, the storm was severe, the boat was *swamped* and it was sinking.

From a problem, we now see an *urgent plea*. The urgency can be seen in that it came from *scared sailors*. The severity of circumstances can at times, be best understood by those assessing the situation. Sometimes the reaction can be under emphasized. Remember Apollo 13? In that instance, a four day ordeal to recover three American astronauts from a crippled spacecraft began with, "Houston, we have a problem." In the case of the disciples, the plea of verse 38 was, "Master, carest thou not that we perish?"

We must remember the disciples were made up of *serious* and *seasoned* sailors. John 21:1-11 verifies they went back to the comfort of their past lifestyles when faced with the reality Jesus would no longer be present with them in the flesh. As you may recall, Jesus called Peter and Andrew from casting their nets for fish in Matthew 4:18 to promising He would make them "fishers of men" (Matthew 4:19). So, while fishermen, some of the disciples had been on the water for most of their lives. As their livelihood depended on knowing, not only how the weather influenced the fish, but how it could endanger the fishermen, they understood issues that would affect their lives and livelihood.

Being *serious* and *seasoned* fishermen they would not only be aware of the possibility of storms, but know how to avoid them as well. As a pilot, part of my responsibility is to check the weather and its possible impact on a flight. Generally speaking, smaller general aviation aircraft cannot climb above the clouds associated with a summer storm like the one I described previously, as the aircraft are not capable of reaching the necessary altitudes. Additionally, circumnavigating, aviation speak for flying around a storm, may be a possibility but may not be a viable reality as it may encompass too large an area. Thus the alternatives for aviators, just as for these seasoned fishermen, are limited. For aviators we can turn around, for the disciples in a small fishing vessel, their only alternative may have been to buckle up and hunker down.

Just as aviators today, the disciple fishermen were equipped to understand the weather and it appears, in this case, they were caught unaware of the possibility of a sudden impending storm. We, like them, no matter how serious or seasoned we are in Christ, how aware we are of our circumstances, or how much planning we have done, sometimes sudden storms befall us and threaten to swamp our lives.

When faced with diversity, it is our responses the world looks to as a measure of what Christianity is all about. You have probably heard the saying, "circumstances make the man." Adding to this, as

I am prone to do on a majority of sayings, issues or topics, I contend circumstances do not make the man-"they reveal the man." What is exposed on the outside should be product of the core Christian convictions we harbor on the inside. We have seen the disciples' urgent plea, directed to a Savior who was slumbering. We are now about to see what a sudden storm reveals about the men.

An initial issue on which we can only speculate is what did the disciples do/not do prior to awakening the Lord. We are not told if they tried to fight the storm or flee. In my imagination I can see them doing both. As noted before, I am a pilot, not a mariner, but fighting by adjusting the sails, moving people around to keep the boat steady, bailing out the water, tacking as necessary, slowing the boat's forward motion (I think this is referred to as "heave to"), could all be viable and reasonable actions to save a sinking boat and may have been done by the disciples. The latter could be considered running from the storm, which would have been a possibility as well.

Sometimes when faced with storms of our own making a 180° turn is the most prudent option. In fact, that, as related to our sin, is the very definition of repentance. The storm the disciples are facing was not self-induced, so repentance is not the issue, but even in sudden storms, turning around is always a viable option. Obviously, this is all conjecture, as to their option, but I can attest, that when faced with the sudden storms in my life, my first response was to attempt to deal with the situation myself. I like to think I addressed the situation using the gifts, talents and wisdom God has given me. Honestly, I do not know if that approach is spiritually correct or not. The attorney side of me could reason learning how to handle present situations based on what God has taught me in the past is the very definition of spiritual growth. Yet, the counter is we should always go to Jesus at the first sign of a storm. Too often Jesus is my last resort as opposed to my first option. Whether we exercise option one or option two and even though Jesus may have been slumbering, we can be conclusive on this point, He was in the boat, exactly where He is in our lives.

We have already seen the disciples' plea. From verse 38 we see the Lord is in a place-in the stern of the boat, in a peaceful *sleep*, with His head on a pillow. There have been times in my walk with Christ where He and I were not in the same place spiritually, so to speak. Do not misunderstand, I am not saying our relationship had been severed as that is not spiritually correct, but I am saying it can be strained based on separation. The Word says in Hebrews 13:5, He (Jesus) will never leave us or forsake us, but we can leave Him and forsake Him. It should be stressed also, we have the indwelling of the Holy Spirit as well, and as such we take Jesus everywhere we go, but even as to our relationship with Him, it is not how much of Jesus I have, but how much of me He has.

There are too many times when we want Jesus working in the emergency, but have not been walking with Him daily, monthly, or yearly. There is a joke you may be familiar with that illustrates proximity and presence. A husband and wife are riding in their truck, the husband driving the wife on the passenger side, discussing their relationship over the years.

The wife laments she used to sit close to him as he drove, he put his arm around her, held her hand and concludes the conversation by generally discusses how things used to be. The husband listens, weighs her comments and finally asks – "Who moved'? Now, remember this is a joke, but I can relate it to my walk with the Lord. Sometimes, too often probably, when looking for Jesus in an emergency I have moved in relation to my proximity to Him. Praise be to God, He is always present. Jesus sought me when He saved me. I should seek Him when in a storm.

Now in verse 39 Jesus *displays His power*. Remember all those words ending in "ing" (sowing, reaping, explaining, lighting, hiding, producing) I used above to highlight the parables in Mark Chapter 14 Jesus had previously taught? The one related to these verses and this storm is *calming*. *Confronting* the elements, Jesus authoritatively, convincingly and with great finality, tells the wind to shutdown and the seas to lay down. The King James Version of the Bible I use says Jesus "rebuked" the wind, but said "peace" to the sea. Rebuke is a very strong word. In

In Malachi 3:11 God says he will rebuke the devour, in Zechariah 3:2 the Lord said unto Satan, "[T]he Lord rebuke thee." Jesus, in Matthew 17:15 rebuked the devil in a child. In Mark 8:32-33, we see Peter rebuking Jesus for discussing His (Jesus') death and Jesus rebuking Peter and says specifically to him, "get thee behind me Satan." In this instance, related to the storm on the sea, as the devil is the "prince of the power of the air" as declared by Ephesians 2:2, it could be argued Jesus' rebuke may well have been directed to Satan himself.

Satan may have been the instigator or could possibly been the benefactor had Jesus not intervened, but this is certain, Jesus was the Master and a rebuke from Him, stopped the wind. Jesus then says to the sea, "Peace be still" (Mark 4:39). Notice, it was the wind that caused the waves. When the wind ceased, the waves were calm. Jesus conquered the wind and *calmed the sea.*

That is my testimony as well, Jesus goes to the source of my storms, rebukes them for my sake resulting in calming, of which I am the benefactor. As glorious as this calming may have been, the ordeal, or at least its consequences and lesson is not quite over and goes beyond the storm.

In verse 40 Jesus gets to the questions we all face when dealing with the storms of life and He does so in a manner that only He can when He asks, as to fear, "[W]hy are ye so fearful?" and also makes it a question of faith by adding, "[H]ow is it that ye have no faith?" (Mark 4:40). Combining His responses to the disciples and speaking directly to us as well, Jesus focuses on our fearfulness as directly related to our faithlessness. From the outset, looking at this as openly and honestly as possible let me say in no uncertain terms, this is very challenging.

As to the issue of their *fear*, should they have not been fearful? I can only speak for myself, but in my experiences when I have asked for Jesus to intervene in whatever the circumstance, and even though I know He can, I am not sure He will as I am not privy to His omnipotence as to the best course for my life. However, even though I know He only has my best in mind, unfortunately it does not mitigate my fear.

So, in the larger context, I like to think I am more faithful than fearful. I will say this; there is a difference between being frightened and being fearful. Fright is immediate and may temporarily immobilize you. Fear is more permanent and will incapacitate you. In the case of the disciples, their initial fright appeared to have escalated to permanent fear. With His answer, Jesus would have dealt with their present fear, but that still leaves the faith issue.

On one side you could honestly ask how were the disciples faithless and how did their lack of *faith* manifest itself? Should they have just ridden out the storm, would that have been an act of faith? Was not their act of faith the fact they went to the Lord as they recognized He was their only hope? The question then becomes, is what Jesus says in verse 40 just that more confusing? Hopefully, it is not. Here He dealt with not only the immediate faith issue, but is looking into the matter of their faith as related to their future. For me the answer lies in verse 41, as the Bible says, "[A]nd they feared exceedingly and said one to another, What manner of man is this, that even the wind and the sea obey him"? Jesus' answer in verse 40 addressed He knew not only the fear they were facing, but how calming the wind and the sea would affect their continuing faith in Him. Do you notice the disciples' puzzlement? It may be one thing to witness how Jesus dealt with sickness, disease, even demons, as in a sense they were more tangible, but to them the elements elevated this to a totally different plain.

Historically, they knew the stories of Moses as he lifted up the "rod of God" in the Exodus account as to the miracles God used to free the Hebrew children.

They understood God had parted the Red Sea to save the Hebrew children from the onslaught of Pharaohs' armies (Exodus 14:16) and even how the armies of Amalek had been defeated as long as Moses' arms remained outstretched during the battle in Exodus 17:10-13. However, to have the wind and sea obey Jesus and to witness it personally was more than they could comprehend. Personally, I can relate to this as well. It is one thing for me to have read and espoused spiritual truth; it is another totally different issue to experience that truth.

Is this not the way we operate as well? In my life I have seen miracles done in matters of health and wealth, but when I need one related to the heart I am fearful and faithless that Jesus can handle that. Too many times I do not look far enough backward to help me look far enough forward. I believe that just because Jesus has not done something for me specifically, does not mean it is not within the realm of his capability, although all to often I am not faithful to my own beliefs. Even in the midst of a miracle, and in the disciples' case, they went from fearing the storm to fearing the Savior. No wonder Jesus says [H]ow is it that ye have no faith?

We also see Jesus can control the wind and the weather as to the earthly, but not the heavenly as related to the will of humanity. Jesus does not insist on coming into the heart, He must be invited. For Jesus to come take residence in one's heart it is an act of faith. The world looks at the Christian and asks how do you have enough faith to believe?

Just as the disciples witnessed the calming of the storm on which to base their faith, humanity has the creation of the universe on which to base theirs. The world looks at the evidence and says they cannot believe in Christ. As Christians looking at the same evidence we say how can we not help but believe. Whatever the conclusion as to belief in Jesus and His provision of salvation of the soul or from the storm, it is a matter of faith and it does not come forcefully, but freely.

There is one final thing we need to speak to regarding this passage and that is the *comforting* effect Jesus has in our lives. Although the passage does not end like this we should not let the story end there. The storm was gone. The moon was up. Just like the sudden storm I encountered and experienced earlier, it dissipated, or in this case, it was dispatched. I understand storms do not necessarily move on or move out in an hour, day, week, month, or sometimes years.

At times and over time, we may continue to fear and possibly fear exceedingly. All that being the case, when the storms of life come, it may take a reminder, or two, or three, but I can be assured Jesus is tenderly asking "why are ye so fearful and [H]ow is it that ye have no faith?" I am confident that our faithfulness in Jesus can, in the present, and will, whatever the future may bring, overcome fearfulness of the storms we will face no matter their suddenness, severity or seriousness.

Chapter Outline

I. Chapter begins with Parables
    A. Sowing and Reaping – the Word
    B. Explaining – the Word
    C. Lighting and Hiding – our Ways
    D. Growing – our Walk
    E. Comparing – our Welcome

II. Chapter ends with a Problem
    A. Storm that is Special – its characteristics
        1. Came up Suddenly
        2. Became Severe
            a. Ship that is Swamped
            b. Savior is Sleeping

III. Urgent Plea
    A. Sailors that are Scared
        1. They are Serious Sailors
        2. They are Seasoned Sailors

III. Jesus Displays His Power
    A. Jesus Confronts the Situation
    B. Jesus Calms the Storm
    C. Jesus Comforts the Sailors
        1. Their Fear
        2. Their Faith

Chapter 3
"What wilt thou that I should do unto thee?"
Mark 10:46-52

Knowing that the Son of God could and would give you whatever you ask of Him, how would you answer this question? Something may immediately come to mind, as it would be necessary to meet a pressing need. It may reflect a long held desire. You may answer not thinking of yourself, but of others. Just these three scenarios represent limitless possibilities. In Mark Chapter 10 we are introduced to a man who was confronted with and challenged by this question. As you look at these scriptures be mindful of not only the conclusion, but also the circumstances surrounding this life-changing question.

This is a familiar passage as it is mentioned in the books of Matthew and Luke as depicting the account of the Lord Jesus' encounter and subsequent healing of the blind man, Bartimaeus. As such, we have a *challenging introduction*, as there are differing biblical depictions of the same event. In Matthew 20:29 the scripture says … "as they departed from Jericho" and in verse 30 the scripture says... "Behold two blind men sitting by the wayside." The Luke account in verse 35 of Chapter 18 the Bible says … "as he came near unto Jericho a certain blind man sat by the wayside, begging." The challenge that Christians face is to reconcile these different accounts.

It is at this point the *skeptic* emphatically proclaims the Bible cannot be trusted as there are so many discrepancies. This is a common refrain from those who want to doubt and find any possible excuse to refute the authenticity of the scriptures. However, I say the *scholar* and I use that term to include every Bible believing Christian, should investigate issues that are presented in different ways.

Now, do I expect to have the same level of expertise that biblical scholars and noted pastors have? No; however, I do expect to put myself in a position to learn by getting into my Bible, submitting to Godly teaching, and supplementing my spiritual education by reading great books and commentaries. Too many times, all Christians know about the Bible is what someone tells them, once or twice a week in a Sunday school class if they attend, or a church service or two – maybe. Yet, we cannot use that as an excuse not to read and study and explore on a personal basis those accounts of events depicted in the Bible, which on their face may appear to be conflicting accounts of the same event.

So, what do we do with these different accounts? First, historically speaking, what do we know about Jericho? We need to recognize this is the same Jericho written of in Joshua 6:20 where the Bible says the "wall fell flat, so that the people went up into the city, every man straight before him and they took the city." So we know one thing for sure-the city was destroyed, so something was different. By the way, before I leave Jericho you do realize there are three ways city walls can be destroyed. Falling out would be the result of an explosion. If they fell in, that would be an implosion. The last option would be for them to fall straight down. I am fundamental enough in my beliefs to think they fell straight down based on how the Bible says the men entered the city. I just do not see them climbing over debris and rubble to take the city, but then that is me.

While I am here, the *skeptic v. scholar* argument is raised because the skeptic will doubt the destruction of the city in the way the Bible depicts it or argues it never happened. Along those same lines, another favorite skeptic issue is their argument the Red Sea (as depicted in the Exodus 14:2-31 account of Moses leading the Hebrews people to the Promised Land) could never have drowned the Egyptians when, at that time of year, it was only two inches deep? My answer is, if that was all the water there was, the fact God used that miniscule amount to defeat Pharaoh's army is an even greater miracle!

Another example is the account in 2 Kings 6:5-6 where the head of an axe Elisha had borrowed fell into the water, causing him great angst. The Bible says in verse 6, "the axe did swim." Now, the skeptic says, this account is flawed. They assert what the scripture really means is Elisha poked and prodded and finally found it. I assert, iron swims. Ask anyone in the Navy who has been deployed on a battleship, cruiser or aircraft carrier if iron swims! The miracles of God are those instances where God does what only God can do. When confronted with what only God can do, one can be either a skeptic or a scholar.

Back to entering and leaving Jericho. We have already seen where Jericho had been destroyed in the book of Joshua and thus it would have had to be rebuilt. The fact is this was done during the reign of Herod the Great, albeit not on the original site. With this information, we can reconcile the Matthew and Luke account as here in Mark, Jesus could have encountered Bartimaeus while leaving the original site or entering the new one.

The last issue addresses one man as opposed to two as represented by the Matthew account of the event. Without being too simplistic, Bartimaeus by his own action is obviously the more vocal of the two. Another viable explanation is two writers of the same event see and write things in the light of what they wish to convey to the reader based on their experience or reaction to it. I dare say if you and I saw the same event, our accounts would not be the same. If you want to experience this firsthand, go to a trial and hear different witnesses testify to the same event and see how much they do, or do not have in common!

From a challenging introduction, we now move to a *blind man's insight*. In verse Mark 10:47, we are told Bartimaeus hears Jesus of Nazareth is there. Note what Bartimaeus says, "Jesus, thou Son of David, have mercy on me." Without making light of how the crowd identified Jesus, and we know He was identified as Jesus of Nazareth by none other than Jesus Himself in Acts 22:8, I do want to make the point that in this case the people saw His *position of geography*. Yet, see how Bartimaeus in his insight identifies Jesus' *position of royalty* as he identifies Jesus with the royal line of David, as verified by the genealogical account of Matthew Chapter 1.

Many times the world identifies Jesus humanly as a prophet, teacher, or a preacher, and they espouse how He should love all things and in all circumstances, but as related to sin, they fail to recognize His royalty, deity, or holiness. In today's society, people use the same analogies used by those of Jesus' day (which we explored in other chapters). Even here, the crowd knew of Jesus and His radical teaching of forgiveness of sins (Luke 7:47), His stand against the religious establishment (Mark 3:1-6), and probably, and in some cases as related to this account, His performance of miracles (Matthew 14:21). In this context, what the world and Christians for that matter want is the Jesus of the geography and miracles but not the Jesus of royalty and deity. So Bartimaeus saw Jesus for "who He was" not from "where He came." Notice also his response as he cries, "have mercy on me."

Now however, we see the *crowd's indignation* as in verse 48 "many charged him that he should hold his peace." Do you see their *rebuke*? People today tell the Christian to hold their peace. It is okay to believe in Jesus, but do not make a spectacle of yourself. Do not bring your beliefs to the schoolhouse, or to my house for that matter, let alone the boardroom or courtroom, just keep that Jesus stuff to yourself. Now, do not misinterpret what I have said. Should Christians be respectful of those places mentioned above – and the answer is absolutely. The fact is, some Christians can and are spiritually obnoxious and that is not a flattering testimony. Yet, we will be rebuked by the world for a non-compromising testimony and we should understand that is their way of having to face their sin nature.

Bartimaeus, confronting the indignation and rebuke…cried the more a great deal and repeats, "Son of David have mercy on me." Have you ever cried for Jesus to meet a need for yourself, a loved one, or a set of circumstance over which you have no control? Then, have you cried the more?

I remember when Suzanne and our 18-month-old daughter were in a car accident. She called to tell me she was not injured, but that my daughter, Stefanie, had been taken to the local children's hospital. I arrived at the hospital and upon entering the room, found her in a stainless steel crib, which reminded me of a jail cell. The diagnosis was that she had broken the growth plate in her jaw, the ramifications being possible surgeries when she grew older to make sure her jaw on both sides of her face grew at the same rate. I remember looking out the window, into the black of night and began to cry. Through the tears came only one prayer and it started and stopped with one word – God. I repeated God's name over and over. I had cried, and cried the more for the mercy of God. Through the years I have cried, and cried the more just as Bartimaeus did here.

I also believe Bartimaeus also recognized that Jesus might not pass his way again. Unlike those who believe Jesus will always be available for the forgiveness of their sin, Bartimaeus saw this might be his only opportunity. How many times have you heard someone say, "Not today" to Jesus and ultimately they have "no tomorrow." Proverbs 95:7-8,

Hebrews 3:7-8 and Hebrews 3:15 all essentially say the same thing, "[T]oday if ye hear his voice, harden not your hearts." Yet another instance of the insight of a blind man, a point, which should not be lost on us, is our responsibility to share Jesus with our lives and lips, as Jesus may not pass this way again for those with whom we come in contact. Bartimaeus, notwithstanding having no physical sight was spiritually insightful, as well we should be.

Verse 49 begins "[A]nd Jesus stood still." I truly believe a cry for mercy will stop deity. Remember Mark 5:28? In that instance a woman with a blood disorder touched Jesus' garment and was healed. He then turns to the crowd and asks, "W[ho] touched me?" In both these instances, with Bartimaeus and the woman, I believe their cry for mercy, stopped deity. I am also under the conviction when I deserve judgment Jesus gives mercy. When I asked Jesus to forgive me of my sin, as a self-serving, judgment-deserving sinner, He stopped and gave me mercy.

Now, from the crowd's indignation we see their reaction. They go from *rebuke to respect*. Refer back to verse 48. As we looked at above, the crowd charged him to hold his peace. Now in verse 49 as Jesus commanded him (Bartimaeus) to be called, they (the crowd), call the blind man. Saying unto him, "Be of good comfort; rise, he calleth thee."

Do you hold fast to your convictions? When there is an off colored joke, or you are asked to go or do something you know you should not do, how do you respond? Do you hold fast to your convictions? You do realize, the world is always watching. You may be the brunt of jokes or ridicule but when there is a tragedy the rebuke will turn to respect. It may come in the form of - I noticed you attend church, my son has a drug habit will you pray for me? Or my husband is leaving me for another woman could I go to church with you? I have been watching you and you have always been so kind, my daughter is pregnant can we talk? If we stand for Jesus, either in this life or eternity, rebuke will turn to respect.

Ultimately, and this is said with the greatest of conviction, the reward may not come until a person you had never seen comes up to you in heaven and says, had it not been for you they would have not been saved. They had heard from your lips and watched your life and at a time of realizing their need for Jesus as Savior, all those years, they had seen Him in you and it eternally changed their lives. Rebuke initially, respect ultimately. Well-done Bartimaeus!

We now go to *Jesus' inquiry*. In verse 51, Jesus gets to the heart of the matter as He answered Bartimaeus' plea and said unto him, "What wilt thou that I should do unto thee?" In the same verse, notice the response. "[T]he blind man said unto Him, Lord, that I might receive my sight." I do not mean to be irreverent but if I am talking to the Lord and discussing this with Him the answer appears to be pretty *obvious*. Lord, knowing you already know everything, but just to make it clear, if there is anything blind people want, it is to see. So...what is it Lord that you are not understanding about this?

What is not so telling about this setting is Jesus always asks the right questions. Although the answer may be obvious, that may not be the case. When it comes to asking the right questions, we should learn from Jesus and do the same. Ever notice when you are talking to your children and you say they cannot listen to this music or go to that movie, what do they always ask? Mom/Dad, what is wrong with it? The reason they do so is they want to debate. Some Christians, when faced with clear biblical standards want to do the same thing. They would rather debate the word of God as opposed to doing the word (James 1:22-23). It is one thing to have a child or a lost person ask this and we should not be surprised when they do. It is yet another when confessing Christians ask the same what is wrong with it question, it challenges God's standards so they can exercise their own will over the teaching of scripture.

If we were like Christ, we would ask the right questions. In response to the "What is wrong with it question," we should be asking, "What is right about it?" Whether it is the child or Christian asking in an act of rebelling, we should respond by asking the right questions. What is right about going to a movie where nudity is portrayed? What is right about dirty language in a song? What is right about the consumption of alcohol? We would do well to ask the right questions as they place the responsibility on the individual to assess their spiritual convictions or lack thereof. In this instance, just as He always does, Jesus asked the right question.

This question is the right one as to Bartimaeus because it is *personal, probing, and promising*. First, Jesus knows each of us personally. In fact, Matthew 6:8 speaks to our Father knowing what things we need before we ask. It is comforting to know God the Father, God the Son and God the Holy Spirit know me personally.

Whether my issues are material, emotional, spiritual, or in the case of Bartimaeus, physical, God knows and cares for me. Beyond that, He knows and still cares even when I have put myself in questionable or compromising positions.

So…if Jesus were to ask you what he could do for you what would you say? It may be a new job. Only to realize the position takes you from your family or church. Or you want that new house. However, payments mean investing more time at work or the covenants and restrictions means more upkeep so you sacrifice your time yet again. As you read this just think of those who you know have prayed for a certain result. The Lord graciously answers the person's prayer and they get the request they have asked from God. Later you inquire to where so and so is, only to learn they have left the church or they got a divorce or no longer have any interest in the things of God. Bartimaeus is facing the same possibility.

There is also a probing nature to this question. Probing questions go deeper than those things we discussed previously. In my own life, the problem is I have responded to personal questions without regard for their probative nature. Too many times, I have probably made requests of God that have been more selfish rather than selfless. Instead of thinking through an issue, I have responded to my flesh instead of my soul. As did Lot in Genesis 13:10, I have erroneously trusted my eyes for the needs of my heart. Had I understood the probative dimension to God's questions maybe my requests would have been different. Jesus asks not only the right questions, but the right types as well.

At the same time, the question could be perceived as being *objectionable*, with an outcome that could be *offensive*. So the question for Bartimaeus is, do you really understand what you will see? At this point in his life, he has probably heard people talking and arguing about race or religious matters but now he is going to see bigotry, prejudice and man's inhumanity to man in ways he could never have imagined.

When my son was younger, much, much younger in fact, he said the word breast. I asked him what that meant and he honestly did not know. He was totally innocent at this point, but as he grew older he, as do we all to some extent, lost that innocence. Like my young son, Bartimaeus' innocence, based on his blindness is going to be exposed to the *objectionable*, which can lead to the *offensive*. So, Jesus asked a personal, probing question. I wonder of myself how I would answer this question if Jesus were to ask me. I would hope I understood the ramifications and would answer in a way that would glorify and edify Christ.

Note also, the question is asked in a way that is also *promising*. When Jesus says we can ask, we can do so expecting an answer. The Bible has numerous examples of Jesus telling us how, when and where to ask. Why would He have immortalized those promises in His word only to not answer our prayers and give us our request? Jesus is not a bait and switch artist. What He promises, He fulfills. How Jesus answers and meets our needs is a subject for another book, but as simplistic as it may be, God answers prayer, and it cannot be disavowed or discredited. As for those who attempt to, I can give personal testimony to God's faithfulness pertaining to my answered prayer. Here, Jesus does not ask, only to say He was just kidding and has no intention of ministering to him, as we see in verse 52 Bartimaeus receives his sight. Instead of leaving him where he found him, helpless and hopeless, Jesus healed him.

Last, we see in verse 52 *faith's illumination*. Bartimaeus receives his sight and the world is now illuminated. Bartimaeus goes from seeing the light of day, to seeing Jesus the light of the world. After years of darkness, Bartimaeus will now be sensitive to the light. We should be sensitive to the light of Christ. Can you imagine how bright the light was to Bartimaeus? Jesus should be that bright to us. Is He still bright to you or have you put on spiritual sunglasses? Have you gotten use to this sin or that sin since you put on those spiritual sunglasses? Are your and my worship, service, fellowship, and Bible study still as bright as they once were? It should be and our responsibility is to make and keep it that way. Jesus sheds light in dark places on dark things. Bartimaeus life has a new light and Jesus was the source.

Not only is there illumination, but there is *direction*. The scripture says he…followed Jesus on the way (Mark 10:52). You do realize direction has a positive and negative aspect. The positive aspect, as here are, Bartimaeus followed Jesus where He was going. We can rest in the knowledge Jesus will only take us to places of blessings.

However, there is another facet as there are places where we should not go or take Jesus there. If you have accepted Christ as savior, you have the Holy Spirit of God living in you (1 Corinthians 6:19) and as such we take God everywhere we go. Remember the children's song that speaks to being careful of your eyes, hands, and feet? Many, far too many times we take God places he had no intention of going and would not have gone but for we took Him. As Bartimaeus, we should follow Jesus as He is always going in the right direction, as is His way.

Jesus will also be a source of *inspiration*. Related to direction is inspiration. If we are following Jesus, we should aspire to do great things for Him. Please understand the context of my using the idea of greatness. An example of greatness is faithfulness. In the parable of the talents Jesus acknowledged as much when He said, "[W]ell done, thou good and faithful servant." Yet, have you been inspired of God to teach a class, or work with teenagers, or pray for someone, or contact visitors or new members, or just be whatever God has called you to do or be? Those are examples of greatness to which God can inspire us. Jesus is the source of inspiration that moves people from the ordinary to the extraordinary. He inspires people that are characters to become people that have character.

One last point as it pertains to illumination, direction, and inspiration. Did you notice Mark 10:50? It says Bartimaeus "cast away his garment." The bottom line is he lost his shirt, but gained his sight. In Genesis 39:12 Joseph lost his cloak, but keep his character. The Samarian woman in John 4:28 leaves her waterpot but becomes as witness. The lesson for you and me is when we give up something for Christ, He gives back.

Having looked at the implications and ramifications of this passage, what wilt thou that Jesus should do unto thee?

Chapter Outline

I. A Challenging Introduction
   A. Viewing the Scripture as a Skeptic
   B. Studying the Scripture as a Scholar

II. A Blind Man's Insight
   A. Seeing Jesus Geographically
   B. Seeing Jesus Royalty

III. The Crowd's Indignation
   A. From Rebuke
   B. To Respect

IV. Jesus' Inquiry
   A. Its Potential
      1. It is a Personal Question
      2. It is a Probing Question
      3. It is a Promising Question
   B. Its Problem
      1. The Answer appears Obvious
      2. The Answer may lead to the Offensive
      3. The Answer may lead to the Objectionable

V. Faith's Illumination
   A. Bartimaeus has new Direction
   B. Bartimaeus has new Inspiration

Chapter 4
"Why callest thou me good?"
Luke 18:18-30

As we study this chapter, it is going to be in a bit of a different format than the others. Here the question of, "why callest me thou good" is in the beginning of the text we will be studying, but first we are going to look at the story and then come back to the question. Like every encounter in which Jesus is involved, there are very practical lessons you and I can glean from it. From what appears to be a person who, by earthly and heavenly standards, would be a candidate for eternal life, the rich young ruler would surely be the one. Yet, Jesus sees and knows better than we do and shows not only us, but the rich young ruler God's standards are not our own as we will see in the context of, "why callest me thou good?"

The account of this incident is also recorded in the gospels according to Matthew in Chapter 19 and Mark Chapter 10. If you read them you will see the term "ruler" is not used to identify the person, but the account as to the circumstances are the same in each of the gospels. So, as we discussed in a previous chapter, remember the skeptic may want to refute the accuracy of the Bible, but you as the scholar can handle the challenge!

Nonetheless, a ruler, in Jesus' time, suggested they were a person of power or having authority. More likely than not they would have been educated in the arts and sciences, politically and or religiously connected, or was economically well off. This being the case, they would have stood out from the crowd either by the entourage around them, the way they were dressed, or by recognition from the crowd. The reality of the situation is we see someone who is *socially commendable*.

Begging your indulgence, and in all humility I am going to use myself as an example of a person who may be considered socially commendable. In describing myself, I am by vocation an academic as a college professor. Additionally, I am an attorney. At this point, you may be saying, there is nothing socially commendable about that! Anyway...I am also an aviator and finally, I am an author. I am also an apologist as I believe the Bible is the inspired Word of God (2 Timothy 3:16).

All those attributes could possibly be considered acceptable and applauded as being commendable in today's society. These are descriptions of "who I am," but they do not describe or provide for, "what I need." Luke 18:18 does, as the ruler asks Jesus about eternal life. You will note, the inference regarding eternal life is in relationship to where one will spend eternity, not to the reality of one living forever. As we see in the world's standards, society looks to commend ability, but Jesus looks at acceptability The argument can be made the ruler saw himself as being spiritually commendable as well. To do so, he looks to the only standard he knows, the Ten Commandments.

Before we look at applying them to the ruler, let's look at what they are. The first four describe our relation to God. To paraphrase, we are to have no other god, nor worship graven images, so this looks at the issue of our <u>loyalty</u>.

Next, we should not use God's name in a vain manner, as defined by being worthless, of no significance, or of no value, and as such we should think of and use God's name, <u>reverently</u>. Honoring our father and mother should be done <u>respectfully</u>. Not killing/murdering should cause us to act <u>humanly</u>. To not commit adultery should compel us to look <u>purely</u> upon our sexual and marital relations. Not stealing is rooted in commending us to live <u>unselfishly</u>. If we do not bear false witness, we will be speaking <u>truthfully</u> in regards to others. Finally, we will live <u>contentedly</u> if we do not covet the intimate or personal possessions of others.

Using the above as a backdrop, we can look further at the notion of being *spiritually commendable*. Looking purely at the numbers, the rich young ruler's average, on a spiritual scale is fifty percent as he acknowledges five of the Ten Commandments he has kept. You could also argue, he only answers the ones Jesus specifically directs to him and by inference, he is saying he has kept the others as well.

So, at first blush he is, a "good" Jew. Taking a closer look and based on Jesus' comments to follow, there may be a problem. Above, I referenced the ruler contends he has faithfully kept five of the ten. Just as I do when challenged by Jesus regarding my attempt to evaluate my spirituality, or lack thereof, or to address a spiritual shortcoming, I grade myself of a scale weighed in my favor. With that in mind, let's look at being spiritually commendable.

As I did with being socially commendable, I am now going to use myself as an example of those times I am spiritually commendable. Let's see, I accepted Christ at the age of seventeen and at the point I could drive myself, I have faithfully attended church. My service in the church has included teaching in such ministries as high school, youth camp (including being a counselor), college and career, couples, what we used to call training union, and substitute taught in various other Sunday school classes. Further, I wrote a book on the basic tenets of the Southern Baptist faith. Moreover, I have served as a deacon in two different and distinct church ministries, and the crème de la crème; I have been a faithful tither.

So...what do you think about that? Pretty spiritual huh? If only I was to use that list, it has to show I have been faithful to a number of scriptural teachings. To do all those things I must have been reading and studying (my Bible), praying, witnessing, outreaching, counseling and tithing. What more could I have possibly done to prove I am a "good" Christian, and as such spiritually commendable?

In fact, all that going on about myself only truly shows, I can be *spiritually conceited*. You see the same is true of the ruler as depicted in verse 21 of this account. After Jesus confronts him with a partial list of the commandments, the ruler proclaims, "[A]ll these have I kept from my youth up" (Luke 18:21). At first blush, the ruler and I may honestly be able to contend we have not committed adultery, at least on a physical level. The same could be said for not killing, stealing or lying about anyone as it has a physical element to it. Spiritually however, there is a conflict. Jesus, coming to fulfill the law, (Matthew 5:17) raised the spiritual bar, so to speak. As to adultery, Jesus said if you look on a woman to lust after her you have committed adultery in your heart (Matthew 5:28).

In Matthew 7:21-22 Jesus deals with all the issues of Luke 18:20 as he says, "for out of the heart proceed evil thoughts, murders, adulteries, fornications, murders, thefts, false witness, and blasphemies." What starts as basically legal physical admonitions prescribed by the law are elevated to spiritual admonishments.

Another trap is that of doing those things that are *spiritually convenient*. All the things mentioned above are things I should be doing for the cause of Christ. I realize this is not quite the same context as this passage of scripture, but the premise is the same. When Jesus spiritually challenges me, I tell Him what I am doing or have done instead of responding to what He is calling me to do. Also, and do not miss this, what I am called to do is not what you are called to do. As the body of Christ, members have been given different gifts to use and different ground to peruse. What we must be cognizant of, just as in the case of the ruler is if we allow it to be, is doing those things that are *spiritually convenient* will justify *the commandments selected*; however, it will also reveal *the commandments neglected*.

A closer look at the commandments Jesus asked of the ruler exposes what is going to be, literally, the heart problem the ruler faces. In a previous chapter, I touched on this, but am going to look at it one more time. The first issue lies in God's first commandment, which as Exodus 20:3 emphatically says, "[T]hou shalt have no other gods before me." When Jesus tells the ruler in Luke 18:22 to, "[S]ell all that thou has, and distribute it to the poor, and thou shalt have treasure in heaven; and come and follow me," the first of the Ten Commandments was in play.

Remember I said there was a heart problem? Jesus with surgical accuracy just went to the ruler's heart, for out of it come the issues of life (Proverbs 4:23). The root question was, do you love the what or do you love the whom? This should come as no surprise as it is seen early on in the lives of the Israelites. Historically, as depicted scripturally, the commandment to have no other gods before God was broken by the Israelites as Moses was coming off the mountain after having received the law.

You know the story. Losing patience with God, in Exodus 32:1-6, the people asked of Aaron, [U]p, make us gods, resulting in the making of the golden calf (Exodus 32:1). Actually, they broke the first two commandments at the same time. They worshipped another god and did it in the form of a golden calf. The result being, they broke the commandment of Exodus 20:3 as well as the one of Exodus 20:4 which says, "[T]hou shalt not make unto thee any graven image, or any likeness of anything that is in heaven above or that is in the earth beneath, or that is in the water under the earth."

It would not be too difficult to say this commandment applies to the ruler as well. In

Luke 20:19-26, the Herodians confront Jesus regarding the issue of paying tribute. In His defense Jesus asks to see a denarius (Luke 20:24). He then queries as to whose image is on it and they respond it is Caesar's. As applied to the ruler, as his wealth was undoubtedly represented by actual money, as in coinage, the unmentioned second commandment was perhaps a point of conviction for him as well.

The last commandment, regarding riches would have been the tenth. I do not want to be too liberal with my interpretation of Exodus 20:17 as related to coveting those things of thy neighbor, but you could reasonably infer the ruler coveted his own riches. As to the confrontation with Jesus, he wanted to keep what he had. He did not necessarily need what others may have possessed, but in a sense, he coveted his own belongings. Biblically this concept is also illustrated in Luke 12:11-21. There was a man who had so much he needed to build bigger and bigger barns to hold his crops only to die in the night and not ultimately able to take his ease and [E]at, drink and be merry (Luke 12:19). So, you ask, what is the point? The point is, the ruler was *sorrowfully confronted*.

Up until Luke 18:24 there is a certain familiar feel to this meeting with Jesus. The scripture identifies a certain person asking a spiritual question and Jesus responds by giving his spiritual counsel and personal charge. As you continue the account, Luke 18:23 adds an important fact and everything takes on a different perspective resulting in a change, from which come enormous consequences.

In Luke 18:18 it says a certain ruler. In verse 23, we see he was "very rich," thus the common description of him as the rich young ruler. Luke 18:22 shows the *challenge* Jesus lays before him. Luke 18:22 also shows his *chagrin* the ruler experiences at the thought of selling "all that thou hast." Taken together, Luke 18:22 and 23 show his sorrow as the scriptures expressly say he was very sorrowful; for he was very rich. For the rich young ruler, the conflict is, will his soul have priority over *his sorrow and his stuff*.

Since my conversion, I have heard many Bible teachings and sermons related to those who are rich. The usual circumstances and analogies are always made. How those who are financially secure cannot relate to their need for spiritual security. How, due to their financial status they do not need to rely on anyone, deity or otherwise to provide for any of their needs. They can buy physical and relational comfort, as well as emotional counsel. The ultimate conclusion becomes, if they can see it, smell it, taste it, feel it, hear it, and they can buy it, then why the need for a Savior?

In verse 24 Jesus recognizes the difficulty of the rich when he says, "[H]ow hardly shall they that have riches enter into the kingdom of God"! Then in verse 25 Jesus analogies the problem using a camel going through the eye of a needle. There are a couple interpretations of the difficulty a camel would have going through the eye of a needle. First, one could think of a literal sewing needle. So that would be obvious. Then there were the gates leading into a city. There were the great gates that were opened during the day for the masses of people and property. Once they were closed, the little gates or needle's eye were used during the night. Conceptually you can think of it as a door within a door. Bible scholars generally believe the reference Jesus is making is to the gate, but if you think about it either one works.

As camels were pack animals, to get through the eye of the needle they would have to be unloaded. In some instances, due to the needle eye's lack of height, the camel would need to be coaxed or prodded to lower its head to get through. As related to the unloading, it is the encumbrances the camel would have to shed to get through the eye of a needle that makes the story so vivid. To unload the camel would be an inconvenience, a hindrance and an impediment.

These are the same issues those who are financially self-reliant have to reconcile when face-to-face with Jesus. Jesus understood, and the rich young ruler knew, he would have to get through the encumbrance of the self-sufficiency to inherit eternal life. By not being able to deny himself, take up his cross and follow Jesus (Luke 9:23), he was ultimately *spiritually condemned* (Luke 18:24-25). Unfortunately, the conversation the rich young ruler has with Jesus starts with *Good Master but ends in Goodbye.*

As the discussion with the rich young ruler is now over there has been some who have been watching and listening (Luke 18:26) to the discourse between him and Jesus. From it, they come up with what may be considered *salvation's conflict*. From their observation comes a reaction and a remark wrapped up in one statement as they ask, [W]ho, then, can be saved?

In the context of what they have heard, the ruler was a pretty good candidate for salvation. He knew the law and kept the law, albeit as we have seen, maybe not all but nobody is perfect. He also has financial resources and even if he did not give them up, he would probably give something to the ministry. Besides, he could be brought along for his counsel and to influence others to bring some money into the coffers for the work of Christ. They may have gone so far as to think (which will be said later), giving up everything to follow Jesus may not be all we thought it would be. All that being the case, as we have already explored, the answer lies in the fact that, "man looketh on the outward appearance, but the LORD looketh on the heart (1 Samuel 16:7).

Jesus then puts their one-sentence question to rest in a likewise one-sentence answer. "[T]he things which are impossible with men are possible with God" and thus reveals *salvation's champion* (Luke 18:27). The miracle of salvation is God's and His alone. He conceived, convened, completed and consecrated it through the Lord Jesus Christ and that is the beginning and the end of the issue. This whole passage shows you cannot be spiritual enough or rich enough to merit salvation.

There is however, the other side of that coin in that you can be bad enough or poor enough to merit salvation and Thanks be to God! Hebrews 12:2 puts all this in perspective as we, in our sinful state, can "look unto Jesus the author and finisher of our faith; who for the joy that was set before him endured the cross, despising the shame, and is set down at the right hand of the throne of God."

One last point before we move on to answer the question included in this passage and that is we see *supernatural compensation*. Peter, in Luke 18:28 makes his usual, "what about us comment," as he feels it necessary to bring something to Jesus' attention.

Here he wants to make it known the disciples have given up everything to follow Jesus. Just to let you know, I do that more times than I care to admit. Then the Lord reminds me, just as he did Peter and all the disciples, if I have left, whatever or whoever for the kingdom of God's sake His blessings on my existing life have been manifold in number (Luke 18:29-30). He promised the same by saying, "The thief cometh not, but to steal, and to kill and to destroy; I am come that they might have life, and that they might have it more abundantly" (John 10:10).

I can testify, God has given me an abundant life. As to my everlasting life, that will be manifold in newness. "Eye hath not seen, nor ear heard, neither have entered into the heart of man, the thing which God hath prepared for them that love him" (1 Corinthians 1:9). Honestly, this statement goes beyond my imagination or comprehension. As I am in the here and now, my references for what heaven may be like are based on an earthly perspective and that is all I have to work with. Heaven is Heaven and I have nothing to compare it to, which makes the above verse so true. I do know this, and rest and glorify in, but if for nothing else, I see Jesus in heaven and that is spiritual compensation enough for me.

With the above as the backdrop, we will now move on to the question Jesus ask in the beginning, "[W]hy callest thou me good?" As you recall this was in response to the ruler in verse 19 asking, "Good Master, what shall I do to inherit eternal life?" When Jesus answers the ruler's question with a question, it is ultimately going to lead the ruler to a spiritual conundrum, one from which he fails to recover.

The first problem the ruler has is one of *perception*. When Jesus answers in verse 19 "[N]one are good, save one, that is God," He has pointed out there is an error in who the ruler perceives Jesus to be. The issue for the ruler is, does he see Jesus as being God or, as he addressed him in verse 18, as a Good Master. We have seen people's perception of Jesus in other scriptures and have discussed it previously, all of which focus on His humanity and not His deity. In this scenario, Jesus points out only God is good and as such does the ruler see Jesus as God, or not. In fact, when Jesus made this statement He reiterates what the scriptures have already said. Psalms 86:5 says, "For thou, Lord are good, and ready to forgive." As to His goodness, it demonstrates God's grace and in forgiveness, as we see His mercy. The Bible says in Psalms 119:68, Thou art good and doest good. This verse simply and concisely says who God is and what He does. The rest of the account leads to addressing another matter the ruler and you and I face as related to goodness.

We have seen the question regarding the *ruler's perception*; we are now going to see the *ruler's perspective*. As we have already seen the ruler presents his arguments regarding why he is a candidate for eternal life. If you remember, we went through what made the ruler a "good" Jew and using myself as an example, we looked at why I may be considered a "Good Christian."

However, looking at the ruler and myself is doing it in the wrong perspective. The right perspective is, just as the perspective the ruler did not see, is are not looking on oneself as *"good"* but raising that standard to be "*Godly* Christians." Before you start jumping up and down and begin pushing back, I understand the connotation associated with being Good Christians and the attributes we assign to them. My intention here is to raise the issue that Jesus raised to make us aware that good is not, or will ever be, good enough and challenge us to a higher standard. If you have not gotten mad at me yet, you may be by the time I finish as we look at the following examples.

I do not know your stand on the drinking of alcohol. There are "good" Christians I know who do drink alcoholic beverages, privately, socially or both. Will drinking send them to hell? Nope. Could it compromise their testimony? Maybe. For example, imagine you walk into a restaurant and see two couples at dinner. One couple is having beer with their meal the other is not. If at that very moment, you were asked which couple you believe to be Christians, whom would you choose?

The answer could be as varied as the number of people who are asked and the answers could, more likely than not be justified, or supposedly so. Your spiritual convictions regarding alcohol are between you and God but as you have seen, I believe it to be a matter of perspective. You may be thinking, he has gone from writing/teaching to meddling and you truly might be correct; but hopefully it is for all the right reasons.

Think about this as I change the scenario. You see someone you know from church coming out of an R-rated movie, the contents of which has been confirmed to have sexually explicit scenes and downright deplorable language. Would you consider them a "good" Christian? Will seeing nude bodies and hearing despicable language send a person to hell? Nope. Do "good" Christians do these things? Probably. Is it Godly behavior? You decide.

Here is the crux of the matter. Just as the ruler told Jesus all he did as related to keeping the commandments, and I exalted my Christian credentials, goodness is the wrong standard. If we go all the way back to Adam and Eve, we see a Godly standard was replaced by a good one. Satan said to Eve in Genesis 3:5, [y]our eyes shall be opened, and ye shall be as God, knowing good and evil. In the end, that is exactly what happened. If you think about it, Satan actually told them the truth! They went from walking with God to hiding from him (Genesis 3:8) as goodness replaced Godliness. See, we recognize the big-ticket items related to evil behavior. So if we are not doing "that" we must be pretty "good." We do the same with our concept of what we consider "good" as opposed to what we should see as "Godly."

If the problem is compartmentalizing our spirituality, which is what the ruler had in recognizing Jesus as Good Master, and not God, then we need to add another compartment. That is just what Jesus did when he asked the ruler the question. Jesus added a new compartment.

By rising the standard to one of being "Godly," He challenged his perceptions and perspective, with one piercing question, "Why callest thou me good?"

Chapter Outline

I. The Ruler is Socially Commendable

II. The Ruler is Spiritually Commendable

III. The Ruler is Spiritually Conceited
    A. Ruler acknowledges those things that are Spiritually Convenient
        1. The Commandments Selected
        2. The Commandments Neglected

IV. The Rich Ruler is Sorrowfully Confronted
    A. He is Challenged
    B. He is Chagrined
        1. Choices
            a. The Rich Young Ruler and his Sorrow
            b. The Rich Young Ruler and his Stuff
            c. The Rich Young Ruler and his Soul

V. The Rick Young Ruler is Spiritually Condemned
    A. From Good Master
    B. To Goodbye

VI. Salvation's Conflict
    A. Disciple's Reaction
    B. Disciple's Remark

VII. Salvation's Champion

VIII. Supernatural Compensation
    A. Existing Blessings are Numerous
    B. Eternal Blessing will have Newness

IX. A. The Ruler's Perception
   B. The Ruler's Perspective
      1. A Question of Goodness
      2. A Standard of Godliness

Chapter 5
"What seek ye?"
John 1:35-42

In this chapter, we will look at when Jesus began to put together his ministry team. Knowing as He does the challenges, controversies, and questions associated with their personal commitments, Jesus begins the recruiting process with a question: "What seek ye"?

Before we look at the question, let's look back at the opening of the book. In John Chapter 1, John (the disciple) begins with the preexistence of Jesus and introduces the ministry of John the Baptist (the Baptist). From verses 15 to 34 the Bible gives an account of John's *proclamation regarding Jesus' deity* (verses 15-19), his *confession of himself personally* (verses 20-26), and his *explanation of Jesus' ministry* (verses 27-34). What should not be lost in this account of his ministry are those who believe in the message John espouses dealing with sin and repentance and their dedication to his ministry all the while looking for the promise of his proclamation of the coming of Christ. It should be remembered those who followed

John (the Baptist) were faithful and loyal. This is illustrated later in Chapter 3 where we see John's disciples in spiritual discussions with the Jews. Later still, after the death of John (the Baptist) at the hands of King Herod the adulterer, as described in Mark 6:29, his disciples came and took up his corpse, and laid it in a tomb. It is against this backdrop Jesus calls his first disciples.

Having looked at the above, even still John (the Baptist) has an additional *observation*. In verses 35-36 of John Chapter 1, the Bible tells us John (the Baptist), standing with two of his disciples declares, "Looking upon Jesus as He walked, he saith, Behold the Lamb of God!" The first thing we should notice about this is the *significance* of his statement. If you notice, John (the Baptist) initially identified Jesus with this exact same phrase in verse 29 adding it is He (Jesus) "who taketh away the sin of the world." So, we have seen this description of Jesus before. Yet, the significance of the statement becomes more relevant when John (the Baptist) says in verse 34, "that this is the Son of God."

The significance and thus relevance of these statements are that in Jesus we see the relationship Jesus had with God as His Son, and the relationship He is going to create with man as Lord and Savior. In one affirmation, John (the Baptist) declares the deity of Christ as God's Son and sacrificially His humanity as God's lamb. In my imagination I can see John (the Baptist) witnessing the descending of the Spirit of God like a dove on Jesus and hearing God declare this is my beloved Son in whom I am well pleased as recorded in Matthew 3:17 and the jubilation that must have brought to his soul. Yet from jubilation,

John (the Baptist) goes to the realization that Jesus is God's sacrificial lamb. It would appear; John's (the Baptist) most lasting impression was seeing Jesus as the Lamb of God and its significance as he must have understood its *symbolism* as well.

The first mention or inference to death in the Old Testament is recorded in Genesis 3:21. Here, God killed one of His animal creations and took the skins to cover His human creations Adam and Eve after they sinned by eating from the tree of the knowledge of good and evil. The term sin offering begins to appear in the book of Exodus and is usually in the context of how Aaron was to conduct the temple ceremony. Rooted in Jewish history, when John (the Baptist) used the term to describe Jesus, the Jews recognized the symbolism. Ultimately, except for a small minority, the Jewish nation did not understand the implications of Jesus being the Lamb of God, but the ceremonial symbolism was ingrained. The fact of the matter is, that may have been their problem. Just as the Jews of yesterday, today's modern day church, me included, recite, respond, regurgitate and sometimes rejoice in manners that are more symbolic than substantive. As we shall see, the scriptures warn of such fallacy.

We read, in Hebrews 9:22, without shedding of blood there is no remission (of sin) but too often do not correlate that with Hebrews 9 verse 28 that so pointedly says, "Christ was once offered to bear the sins of many..." When Philip in Acts Chapter 8 verse 32, referencing Isaiah 53:7 says, "[H]e was led as a sheep to the slaughter; and like a lamb dumb before his shearer, so opened he not his mouth." Symbolism had become realism.

You are probably familiar with the medical concept of a blood transfusion. Generally, for whatever reason, a person may need to be given blood. Normally it comes from someone who has given his or her blood to be used by anyone who may need it, which is a very gracious gesture. Symbolically, this is not what Jesus, as the Lamb of God, did for us. In reality, He was our blood substitution. God the Father required the precious blood of Christ, as of a lamb without blemish and without spot (1 Peter 1:9) to take away my sin. My blood, or the blood given to me by others, with all its impurities would not be enough to pay my sin penalty. In fact, the Bible never mentions a person getting new blood, but the psalmist in Psalms 51:10 does asked God, "to create in me a clean heart."

Paul in Romans 3:25 said it so succinctly when he asserts, "[W]hom God hath set forth to be a propitiation through faith in his blood, to declare his righteousness for the remission of sins that are past..." When John (the Baptist) looking upon Jesus as He walked and said, "Behold the Lamb of God," we can be assured he understood the totality of the spiritual significance and symbolism of what he was saying.

As the account continues, we see that two of John's (the Baptist) disciples had an opportunity to hear Jesus speak and began to follow him (John 1:37). If you are of the age to remember, a well known television commercial of its time announced, "When E.F. Hutton talks, people listen." When Jesus talks, we should listen. Through a pastor talking, the text of the Bible, the testimony of a saint, or the conviction of the Holy Spirit, when Jesus talks we should listen.

Taking that concept one step further, we should do something with what we hear. Here, the disciples physically followed Jesus. Sometimes, what we do may not be that covert or radical. Our following may be a phone call we make, or a meal we take, but we should act when Jesus speaks to us. Back to the disciples' interest, the Bible does not say why they are following, but Jesus notices the disciples and thus we see *Jesus' Attention*.

Admittedly, "What seek ye?" on its face is a simple question. It also does not seem to have any implications other than to ask what the two disciples wanted. Yet, the most innocuous questions can be the most relative and revealing. Notice Jesus asked what, not who. As you can probably attest, people come to Jesus for multiple reasons. In some instances, it is *personal*, in the sense, it is due to wanting to please another. How many testimonies have you heard where the initial reason a person came to Christ was a parent, girlfriend, or whomever? Do not misunderstand, initially those reasons can be the underlying foundation of a lifetime of commitment, but those people, in and of themselves are not enough to sustain the commitment if it is not based in and on Jesus.

Another reason people come to Jesus is based in the *material*. You may be familiar with an older, well a little older, spiritual teaching that if you name it, you can claim it. That philosophy has given way to a prosperity gospel, which says, God wants all Christians to be materially prosperous. Although I am not a proponent of prosperity blessings, in the sense these teach, I am one of provisional blessings. However, let me be very clear on this point, God has blessed my life materially and provided for not only my needs, but also many of my wants. The issue then becomes what if God does not give me all the things I ask for? Is it an issue of faith or lack thereof as some claim? That being the case, do I cut and run? Some people run from Jesus at the first sign of material adversity. Some run to Jesus at the prospect of material prosperity. Thus "what seek ye," though simple, has substantial ramifications.

In fact, we have a Biblical example of the rich young ruler in Luke 18:18-27 (see previous chapter). The circumstances were the man asked what he must do to inherit eternal life. Jesus then went through the commandments to which the man answered he had kept them from his youth (Luke 18:21). When Jesus told him to sell all he had (verse 22) the scripture says in verse 23 he was "very sorrowful, for he was very rich." If you notice, Jesus did not mention the one commandment the rich man was in violation of, which is the most imperative of them all...thou shalt have no other Gods before me (Exodus 20:4). Had that one not be so egregious, coveting would have sufficed as well. The point is, some see Jesus for only the material and when that is in doubt or jeopardy, their basis for coming to Christ has crumbled.

Others come to Jesus based on the *emotional*. As you may recall, some in Jesus' day came to Him based on how He made them feel. When those feelings were challenged with the reality of a life centered in Jesus, things changed. We see this very principle illustrated in John 6:30-59. In the verses just prior to these, Jesus had begun by discussing God's provision of manna and ended by His declaration of Himself as the living bread. Then in verse 60 we read, [M]any, therefore, of his disciples...said, "[T]his is a hard saying. This time many of his disciples went back and walked no more with him." Jesus, in verse 67 addresses the twelve and asks, "[W]ill ye also go away?"

In our modern scenario, people come to Christ for the same reason. Maybe they attended a church service and from the very first note of the first song, they sensed spiritual electricity. As the songs continued and the preaching of God's word began, they became more and more caught up in their own emotions and the emotions of those around them. When the invitation is given, they responded and made a decision.

However, in the coming weeks the music is not as emotionally inspiring, the message of God's Word does not seem to speak to them as it originally did. They also are being pressed and pressured by the cares of the world. Where God once seemed to answer every prayer, the answers are not forthcoming any more. Where there was a hunger for God's Word, it has now waned. For them, the Christian life has turned from a playground to a battleground and they are not prepared for the fight, as their emotions have subsided and quite literally, their heart is not in it.

The parable of the sowing and reaping elucidates this most clearly. Jesus, in Mark 4:1-12, introduces the parable and then in verses 13-20 explains it. In discussing the seed, and as you already know is the Word of God, Jesus says some is sown on stony ground and it is immediately receive with gladness (the emotional aspect) (Mark 4:16), but in verse 17 He says it has no root "in themselves." Jesus then continues and says..."and so endure but for a time;

afterward, when affliction or persecution ariseth for the word's sake, immediately they are offended." I may be postulating here, but I contend emotions are an example of the concept Jesus is claiming is a component of being "in themselves." Therefore, coming to Jesus to placate one's emotions may be a strong motivation and I totally understand people have come to Him under emotional circumstances and in some cases, they have been extreme, but is not a solid foundation on which to build a sustaining spiritual life. Emotions are fickle, rising and falling based on the good, the bad, and the indifference and therefor have no root "in themselves."

You may or may not be familiar with the Four Spiritual Laws. This is, or at least was, a witnessing tool used to present a simple plan of salvation. At the end is an illustration of a train with a locomotive pulling two cars. The locomotive was labeled Fact, the other two, Faith, and Feeling. It was there to assure the person they could rely on the Facts as to witness of the scripture as they pertain to sin and salvation and Jesus as Savior. Then by Faith they could come to the saving grace of Christ. The last car on the train was Feeling. The point was, some might experience different levels of emotions as related to their salvation experience. Yet, in order of reliability, it was the last because their salvation was already based in Fact and Faith.

Illustrating it this way, sometimes my wife probably does not feel like she is, or wants to be married to me. Realistically, after some of the boneheaded stunts I have pulled, I would agree with her. Fortunately, for me, we have the fact of a marriage license, which has all the pertinent information and witnesses as well! She then puts her faith in our relationship that it will endure the ups, downs, and all arounds associated with devoting your life to another. So, no matter her feelings, she and I are still husband and wife.

Those who come to Christ so they may feel happy or not feel sad, to be glad or not feel bad will find these emotions may not be able to sustain them when faced with the adversarial challenges and circumstances of life. The issue is not what Jesus does for us emotionally, and He is a comfort in the midst of the storm, but what He ultimately does for us spiritually and eternally. The conclusion to be taken from the above examples is, the "what" that brings people to Christ will not sustain them if they do not know the "who" of the relationship.

Not wanting to leave this section on the negative aspects of why people come to Christ, I do want to touch on the positive. As mentioned above, people come to Jesus because they understand their need for all things spiritual. Just as we looked at Fact, Faith, and Feeling when we look at man's triune nature, we are Body, Soul and Spirit. John Chapter 3 looks at man's spiritual need. There, Jesus addresses the body and the spirit when he confronted Nicodemus with his need to "be born of water and of the Spirit."

As these verses recognize the spiritual birthing, there is also the realization of *spiritual* blessings. In essences, in Ephesians 1:3 it says "God, through Jesus has blessed us with all spiritual blessings in heavenly places in Christ." I can say without reservation and in all aspects, whether in the realm of the personal, material, financial, intellectual, emotional, relational, or vocational all are based on, and in, God's spiritual blessings on my life. Everything of value I have or will recieve, or anything of spiritual value I ever say or do is the direct result of God's blessings of grace and mercy. Not only are there the earthly blessings of today but the heavenly, eternal blessings I will yet receive.

Coming to Christ also has an *eternal* appeal. Honestly, I cannot imagine the eternal blessings of God. Did you know He actually understands my inability in this area as well? In Isaiah 64:4 and 1 Corinthians 2:9 the Bible says, and I am paraphrasing; that my eyes cannot see, my ears cannot hear and my heart cannot conceive the things God has prepared for, and has waiting for me. I understand this verse can be applied to both my natural and eternal life, but in this instance, I am looking at it eternally. In my mind's eye I can see streets of gold, gates of pearl and a mansion He has built for me in glory (John 14:1-6).

Using a pilot example, which I happen to be, what God has for me eternally would be like a person who has been blind from birth trying to describe the space shuttle – there are not enough words and they would not be adequate. When I came to Christ, one of the reasons, which I grasped, was the issue of where I would spend eternity, which was immediately settled. In my spiritual innocence, I immediately understood the where of my eternity, but as I have grown in my spiritual intellect, I cannot grasp the wonder of that eternity, except to say I will be in the presence of the Lord, and to God be the glory.

As we return to the scriptures, whether the next part of the encounter was a means to deflect the question Jesus asked, an attempt to divert the

Lord's attention, or just a declaration of Jesus' authority, I do not know. I do know that before they got to the question they wanted answered, they recognized and respected something about who Jesus was as they called him Rabbi, which is to say being interpreted Master, (John 1:38). We see this particular reference to Jesus in other instances. When done by those who are honestly seeking Jesus, it is meant in greatest reverence.

In other Biblical references, such as the account of the woman taken in adultery, the scribes and Pharisees used the term in defiance and more so, to tempt and test Jesus. Today, people look at Jesus as Master in the same light. Either he is one's Master, or he is a constant reminder He should be, just as He was 2000 years ago.

Now we see the *disciples' investigation*. As we have already discovered, there was a question of what, now there is a question of where. The disciples ask Jesus, in verse 38, where dwellest thou? It is a *simple*, albeit very *practical question*. We know from other scripture text, Jesus did not have a permanent home in the literal sense, except of course, with His parents Joseph and Mary. Other times, as verified by the scriptures, He went into the home of publicans/sinners, disciple Matthew's home (Matthew 9:9-10), the home of Lazarus, Mary and Martha (John 12:1), celebrated Passover in the guest house of an unnamed person (Mark 14:14) and was buried in a borrowed tomb (Matthew 27:57-61). The answer, just as was the question, was going to be as simple as well – Come and see. There, in all its splendor, was Jesus' invitation.

My son went on a recruiting trip to a college that

was interested in him playing soccer for them. While he was there, the coaches spoke to him, a person in the administration's office discussed the academic requirements and a student was assigned to show him the campus and the social aspects of campus life. All this was done in an effort to highlight the best aspects of the college and as a result convince him to come there to play. In essence, they were trying to impress them by putting on their best.

As this was a disciple-recruiting trip, so to speak, ever wonder what they came and saw (John 1:39) as to where Jesus dwelt? We see the answer in Luke 9:58 where Jesus says of himself, "[F]oxes have holes, and birds of the air have nests; but the Son of Man hath nowhere to lay his head."[1] Do you think it could have been a bit of a surprise when they found He had no home? If this were the best Jesus could do to impress them and feature the best aspects of his ministry, this would appear to be lacking. Yet, the disciples abode with him that day (John 1:39).

The key is the blessing was not in the *where*, but in the *who*. For all the simplicity and practicality of asking Jesus where he dwelt, it was the *spirituality* of the question that mattered most. Being where Jesus is, no matter the creature comforts, is where we should want to be, as it is where the blessing are. Above, when I said the college put on its best to recruit my son, Jesus presented Himself to His prospective disciples, and He is His own best recruiter.

In the next part of the narrative, we see a *disciple's*

---

[1] As to this reference, a few years ago a prominent woman in the White House was advocating the plight of the homeless and used Jesus as an example to underscore her argument. One's political views notwithstanding, I am not sure her analogy was in the same context.

initiative and identification. In verse 40, Andrew goes to find his brother, Simon Peter. Something happened in those hours Andrew met with Jesus. Beginning with Andrew's identification, Jesus goes from Master in verse 38 to Messiah in verse 41. The verses expound on this as they say, "Messiah, which was, interpreted, the Christ." In that time Andrew spent with Jesus his level of understanding of who Jesus was, changed. His perspective went from that of Jesus being a teacher, to Jesus being Savior and that is what time with Jesus will do; it will change you.

Finally, we revisit Andrew's initiative. He starts by finding his own brother. There is probably no harder mission field than that of your own family. The reason is they know everything about you and will remind you of it! The result is, you can say whatever you wish about your changed life, but they will be watching and in some cases waiting to see if your conversation and dedication to Christ is genuine.

As hard as it may be and the risk you may take, look at the reward. Andrew found Simon, who we more commonly refer to as Peter. This is Peter, the preacher at Pentecost and the Peter after whom books of the Bible are named. This is the Peter who has impacted the lives of Christians throughout history and into eternity. You see, we never truly know the impact of our witness. Had Andrew never spoken to another person, his initiative was rewarded by speaking to one and it all began when Jesus asked... What seek ye?

Chapter Outline

I. John the Baptist's Assertion
　A. His Proclamation – Jesus' deity
　B. His Confession – of himself personally
　C. His Explanation – of his ministry

II. John the Baptist's Observation
　A. Significance – Jesus, the Son of God
　B. Symbolism – Jesus, the Lamb of God

III. Jesus' Attention
　A. People Come to Jesus for Reasons That Are – Personal
　B. People Come to Jesus for Reasons That Are – Material
　C. People Come to Jesus for Reasons That Are – Emotional
　D. People Come to Jesus for Reasons That Are – Spiritual
　E. People Come to Jesus for Reasons That Are – Eternal

IV. Disciples' Investigation
　A. Simple Question
　B. Practical Question
　C. Spiritual Question

V. Jesus' Invitation

VI. Disciples' Initiative and Identification
　A. Andrew seeks his brother
　B. Andrew introduces the Savior

Chapter 6
"Saul, Saul, why persecutest thou me?"
Acts 9:1-6

In the previous chapter, we saw Jesus call his first disciples. As unmistakable and remarkable as those circumstances were, in Acts 9 we see Jesus recruit arguably the most prolific evangelist of all time. His ministry was commissioned, concentrated, and consecrated by Jesus as, a "[c]hosen vessel unto me, to bear my name before the Gentiles, and kings and the children of Israel" (Acts 9:15). Adding to this is the fact this recruit became an extraordinary writer, authoring thirteen, possibly fourteen depending on whom you ask, of the twenty-seven books in the New Testament. He also had a change in not only his person from Saul to Paul (Acts 13:9) but had a change of position as he went from being a persecutor of the church to an Apostle in the church. All this started by Jesus asking, "Saul, Saul, why persecutest thou me?"

As we begin looking at this person Saul, it would behoove us to get an overall feel for who he was, which will lead us to the stem of the question Jesus asked, addressing the why was he persecuting Jesus.

In Acts 22:3, Saul gives us some insight into *his contempt for the church*. Before moving too quickly, let's define church so we are using the same word from the same dictionary, which sometimes the church and the world do not do. The best dictionary to use to find this definition is the Bible. Here you will find the church is the body of believers who have received forgiveness of their sins through the blood, death, burial and resurrection of Christ. Jesus gave himself (Ephesians 5:25) for the church, sanctified and cleansed it (Ephesians 5:26) nourisheth and cherisheth it (Ephesians 5:29) and will present it to Himself (Ephesians 5:27). There is never a better source than the Bible to define and defend what defines the church. With this backdrop, let's interview Saul and let him tell us about his *parturition, education, premeditation and personal conviction* as they related to his dealings with the church prior to his encounter with Jesus.

Jerusalem Herald (JH): Saul, thank you for taking time to speak with us today concerning your role as you see it regarding how you are dealing with those affiliated with this upstart group called the church (Acts 2:47), its disciples (Acts 9:1) and its founder, Jesus.

Saul: It is a pleasure to be here.

JH: Let's start by looking at your Jewish background to get a feel for why you believe you are qualified to take on this responsibility.

Saul: Absolutely. Actually, I was born for this role. I am a man who is a Jew, born in Tarsus, a city in Cilicia (Acts 22:3). Additionally, I was circumcised the eighth day, of the stock of Israel, of the tribe of Benjamin (Philippians 3:5).

JH: Obviously that establishes your Jewish parturition, but how would you answer your critics who say that in and of itself that is not enough to give you license to persecute people of "this way" unto death, binding and delivering into prisons both men and women (Acts 22:4)?

Saul: Well, not only do I have the requisite Jewish parturition you mentioned, but the proper education as well. I was brought up in Cilicia, at the feet of Gamaliel and taught according to the perfect manner of the law of the fathers and was zealous toward God (Acts 22:3). Gamaliel was a teacher of the law, a Pharisee and a member of the council, a teacher of the law, held in reputation among all the people (Acts 5:34). If you combine the realities of my parturition and education, we just discussed, in essence I am a Hebrew of the Hebrews, as touching the law, a Pharisee (Philippians 3:5). As such, my religious education gives me license to deal with the blasphemy associated with these "Way People." (Acts 19:9, 23).

JH: Some would say there is certain premeditation to the how and the way you have dealt with the followers of Christ. How would you address those making these claims?

Saul: I totally agree. My actions persecuting the church have been done with zeal (Philippians 3:5). As you also are aware, I was consenting to the death of Stephen, where at that time there was great persecution against the church which was at Jerusalem; and they were all scattered abroad throughout the regions of Judaea and Samaria...(Acts 8:1).

JH: Earlier you mentioned Gamaliel, for who you were an understudy. If you remember, at the inception of the church, he advised the council of the Pharisees to take heed to what ye intend to do as touching the apostles (Acts 5:35) and to "[R]efrain from these men and let them alone; for if this counselor this work be of men, it will come to nothing, [B]ut if it be of God, ye cannot overthrow it, lest perhaps ye be found even to fight against God." These statements appear to be in direct contradiction to your actions. How do you reconcile his words and your actions?

Saul: I have great conviction regarding this. Let's look at Jesus and his death on which these upstarts base their faith. The law incontrovertibly says in Deuteronomy 21:23, "[f]or he who is hanged is accursed by God." If Jesus was the Son of God, as claimed, how can they reconcile this dilemma of being accursed? I contend they cannot. Remember also, while Jesus was alive He claimed equality with God when the high priest asked Him, and said unto Him, "Art thou the Christ, the Son of the Blessed"? [A]nd Jesus said, "I am"... (Mark 14:61-62). This, as the high priest rightfully declared, was blasphemy (Mark 14:64). Jesus also made a claim while in the temple saying, "[D]estroy this temple and in three days I will raise it up" (John 2:20). Obviously, that did not happen, as the temple remains intact. So, with great respect to Gamaliel, statements and actions of this nature must be confronted at their inception and not allowed the possibility of taking root no matter how shallow those roots may be.

Based on these three examples and there are countless more, Judaism and the beliefs of these so-called Christians (Acts 11:26) are not compatible. Either one or the other can be true, but not both. On our side, we have a rich heritage as opposed to what appears to be based in heresy. We also have our Jewish culture, which contradicts the claims of a cult. It is for all the things we have already discussed related to my qualifications, and my ultimate commission by those who are in charge of protecting the Jewish nation, I will continue, whether they are men or women to bring them bound unto Jerusalem (Acts 9:2).

JH: Thank you for speaking with us.

Saul: You are very welcome.

Having looked at Saul's past and his contempt for the church we will now look at his present and his *charge against the church*. In Acts 9:1-2 we see where Saul got his authority, that being from the high priest. Specifically, repeating Acts 9:2 above, "[A]nd desired of him (the high priest of Acts 9:1) letters… that if he (Saul) found any of this way, whether they were men or women, he might bring them bound unto Jerusalem."

Actually, there is a question as to who the high priest was at the time of Saul's conversion. Some espouse it is Caiaphas, who Jesus was taken to in John 18:13, 24 as part of his trial before the Sanhedrin. He was also the one who, for political reasons as opposed to a heavenly reason, made this devastating statement, as related to Jesus, that "it was expedient that one man should die for the people" (John 18:14).

Others claim the high priest was Jonathan, the son of Annas. If you remember, Annas sent Jesus to his father-in-law Caiaphas (John 18:13). Still others claim the high priest during Saul's reign of terror was Annas' other son, Ananias. Whoever you believe the high priest to be, it is clear the persecution of Christ from His past, to persecuting His church in Saul's present, the office of the high priest was still trying to eradicate everything associated with Jesus, and that is where Saul got his charge.

As the foundation of the church cannot be quashed, there are still forces trying to *suppress the message of the church*. For example, just as some political entities have proposed legislation against hate crimes, this concept is being expanded to include proposed hate speech. Under this concept, should a pastor preach or teachers teach the Bible's stand on homosexuality they could face possible criminal charges.

As an attorney, I would argue this has serious first amendment challenges, but that is not the point. The emphasis is there are forces that want the church to abandon its core beliefs as related to what God considers sin. Under the concept of hate speech the problem becomes speaking against adultery, premarital sex, abortion, stealing or lying could be considered hate speech. I would counter, when speaking against issues of this sort, it is not hate speech, but "love speech." The church is responsible to teach "[F]or all have sinned and come short of the glory of God" (Romans 3:23) "[F]or the wages of sin is death but the Gift of God is eternal life through Jesus Christ our Lord" (Romans 6:23) and to not do so would actually be a hate crime. The church is responsible to stay on point as to evangelizing the lost and equipping the saints. To do so, you the church must do everything possible against those forces who attempt to thwart those efforts. When we use the scripture to witness and share Christ, it is not said in hate, but in love. Neither should we let the world define our speech in the negative and of course we should never speak in any way other than in a loving manner.

Forces are also trying to silence the *members in the church*. In Acts 9:2 you will see the phrase "any of this "way"" which implies a negative connotation. That same negative inference, is found in Acts 19:9, 23, 22:4, and 24:22 pertaining to people of the/that "way." However there is a very positive side to alluding to those who followed Jesus as people of the "way." I have no basis other than my personal conviction on this matter so take this as you may. Jesus said in John 14:6, "I am the way, the truth, and the life, no man cometh unto the Father but by me." In these verses, we see Jesus is the pathway to God, He is the way. He is the way of truth, philosophically as there is no other practical truth upon which to compare Jesus. He is the way of, and to eternal life, permanently. He also mentioned this way is narrow in Matthew 7:13-14.

In its simplest form, this is the gospel message and the message of the saints. The world attempts to silence this message in the saints. Radical religious groups attempt to do so through murdering Christians. Even Saul consented to the death of Stephen in Acts 7:54-8:1. The world attempts to shout down and drown out the love speech of the Christian as alluded to above regarding abortion, gay rights, euthanasia and evolution. Yet, just as the high priest attempted to use Saul to silence the "people of this way," as we will see, Jesus takes their crusader for evil and converts him to a lifetime of evangelism.

As we continue, in Acts 9:3 we see *the light Saul witnessed*. At first glance, the significance of this might escape us. If you look at Acts 22:6 however, we can see this is no ordinary light as Paul (his name has been changed in Acts 13:9) gives testimony that he saw this light around noon. For a light to outshine the midday sun, it must be quite a light. Jesus is that light. He is the bright and morning star of Revelation 22:16. He is the culmination of the description of day star in 2 Peter 1:16-19. You recall there was a star that led the wise men to the home of Jesus to worship the young child, born King of the Jews (Matthew 2:2). In the most important context of all, Jesus is the light of the world (John 8:12). The sun had no choice but to dim in the presence of the Son of God.

Acts 9:4 exposes the accusation Saul must answer. It also reveals the question we must answer eventually and individually. The first thing to notice is Jesus takes personally the attacks on His children. Saul had never seen Jesus, much less persecuted Him. He had persecuted people individually, as regarding Stephen, and collectively as described previously in Acts 9:1 and revisited by Ananias in Acts 9:13. This persecution did not go unnoticed by Jesus and He said it to Saul and at the same time says it to us.

The abusive accusations, actions, or attitudes you and I have to deal with from the unsaved and in some cases, those espousing to be believers are something Jesus takes notice of and is attuned to. Whether the persecutions come from worldly philosophies, politicians, or people, Jesus will have the last word and his judgment on our behalf will be final and fatal. "Vengeance is mine; I will repay, saith the Lord" (Romans 12:19) is a principle by which we can live and a promise Jesus has made to those who have persecuted

Him, through their actions against His people.

We now see Saul is looking for an answer as he asks in Acts 9:5, "[W]ho art thou Lord?" Admittedly, there may be an issue of specificity as to whom this lord is Saul has encountered, but he knows one thing, there is something supernatural about this confrontation. I advocate Saul knew it was Jesus. As we have seen in a previous chapter, Jesus knows how to ask the right questions. He did not ask Saul any of the questions we have already addressed. The question was not about Jesus and his identity. Not about Jesus and his ability. There was not issue as to Jesus and eternity. Nor did it deal with faith, fear, or the future.

The issue to be answered here concerned tyranny. Saul had already admitted how and upon whom he had exposed his laser focused, religiously sanctioned wrath and zeal. It was on those professing and living the teachings of Jesus. Saul understood the connotations of the word persecutest. Whether historically through the words of the Old Testament or his experience with an oppressive Roman government meted out by corrupt governors and officials, some with Jewish roots, Saul understood the meaning of persecutest as related to the accusation made by Jesus.

Just in case there was any doubt as to whether Saul knew it was the Lord of the universe, it will be eliminated with the acknowledgement, "I am Jesus whom thou persecutest." (Acts 9:5.) If you look at the first two words of that statement, you may be reminded of its use in Exodus 3:12 when God responded to Moses by identifying Himself as, "I

AM THAT I AM." As God is the I AM of the Old Testament, Jesus is the I AM of the New Testament and just as God knew Moses, Jesus knows Saul.

Looking at the next statement gives us a hint that this was not the first instance Jesus was trying to get Saul's attention. Note what Jesus adds in Acts 9:5, "it is hard for thee to kick against the goads." In your Bible, as in mine, the word "goads" may have some type of parentheses around it. Generally, this means the translators have inserted a word in place of another. In my Bible, goads was inserted instead of pricks. I like the substitution as it brings to mind the idea of someone goading another into doing something.

You are probably familiar with the concept, as you have probably done it a time or two to your friends, most likely culminating in them doing something that ends up embarrassing themselves. Another word associated with goading would be to prod. A way to visualize this would be thinking of someone wearing spurs while riding a horse. The rider needs to not only get the horse's attention, but also add some additional incentive for it to do the rider's bidding. The spurs add the incentive, as well as doing a little coaxing! Jesus' statement infers He had been attempting to get Saul's attention. This could have been evidenced in a number of ways. I have no doubt Saul had seen the sincerity of those who had come to Christ. More likely than not he had also witnessed their steadfast dedication to their Messiah. Everything Saul saw and did was not done in a vacuum, as he witnessed how the saints responded to his attempt to compel them to blaspheme the Lord and when they did not he punished them for being true (Acts 26:11). I believe Saul had been and was being goaded by these instances.

Having said the above, do not misunderstand my perspective. The Lord does not beat people into believing. He knocks on the door of people's hearts, but does not knock those doors down (Revelations 3:2). I believe in a Lord that softly and tenderly calls.[2] Even as related to Saul's present revelation, Christ asked a question but made no demands. In our lives, He has done the same. Jesus asks is that the person you really want to be? Is that the life you want to live? Is that the eternity you want to endure? Sometimes in the life of the lost, what may bring the revelation of Christ's call may have been done dramatically as exemplified by the death of a loved one, the breakdown or break up of a marriage, or the heartbreak associated with the actions of a child. As in the atrocities Saul heaped on the called of Christ, today people come to Christ due to violent circumstances they have experienced in their lives or they have seen in the lives of others, but Jesus comes to heal in the face of the hurt. Just as He does today, Jesus calling to Saul was done in tenderness, not to terrorize.

In response to the conversation, we now see *Saul's conversion*. Where he was inquiring before, the reality of the situation and who he has been talking to and the ramifications associated with a personal encounter with Jesus now has him trembling (Acts 9:6). There may be a little bias in what I am about to say and if so, I hope it not offensive. But there are two areas

---

[2] In his song Softly and Tenderly (published 1880) Will L. Thompson wrote: Softly and tenderly Jesus is calling, Calling for you and for me. To see the complete lyrics go to www.timelesstruths.org and click through the available links.

in today's Christian world where there is a lack of trembling. The first relates to the church. The world no longer trembles at what the church stands for.

The answer could well be because in too many churches they stand for nothing, everything or maybe worse do not know what they stand for. Things that would have never been tolerated are now commonplace. Sin is no longer called sin. All lifestyles are tolerated. Anything one wants to do is ok, just make sure it is done in moderation. Marriages are not worth fighting for, as God understands the husband and wife fell out of love. Too many churches no longer set standards or conform to them. The Bible cannot be the standard as it is not consider the inerrant word of God. No longer is the standard infallibility, but philosophy. We have gone from expository preaching to entertaining philosophies. Not taking the teachings of the Bible literally, leads to liberality of thought and action. The result is the world does not tremble at the things of God because the church does not tremble.

If the church collectively no longer trembles, neither do the individuals who make up the church. Just as the physical body, the church body is not going to be any stronger than its collective parts. Those who have experienced salvation have also been called to sanctification, defined by being set apart. Let's say a pastor opens the Word of God and preaches the traps and treacheries of sin. The members are emotionally stirred and leave the service. However, the next day, faced with the opportunity to spread a little gossip, use language even the world would define as filthy, or get physically involved with a coworker they do not tremble at the prospect of impending sin as they have bifurcated their spirituality from their world's reality.

The practical result is God is for Sunday, their will and ways are for every other day. People compartmentalize their spiritual talk and their walk from their actual talk and walk and as Rudyard Kipling, borrowing from the Bible (Psalms 103:12), expressed, neither the twain shall meet. Too many want to hold to the Grace and Mercy of God, but conveniently want to disregard His Holiness. We need to go back to the beginning which literally is, "the fear of the Lord is...the beginning of knowledge" (Proverbs 1:7) ..."the instruction in wisdom" (Proverbs 15:33)..."and the beginning of wisdom" (Proverbs 9:10). Faced with meeting Jesus, Saul was *trembling*; sometimes we/I need a double dose of trembling.

What Saul heard and saw was also *astonishing*. He saw the light associated with the brilliance of Jesus as well as heard directly from the lips of Jesus. A life that you and I may have eliminated for all its transgression against Christ was now going to be elevated to do great things for Him. Personalizing this, at the end of this book, as was in my first, is my testimony. As you read it I hope you will see what Jesus did and continues to do for me was, and is, astonishing. By just being everything He said He would be, my needs have been met as well as many of my wants. He has freed me to be all I can be in Him. I am far from everything I should be, but that is based in my sinful nature as a person, but not based on the potential God has for me. Astonishing, amazing, astounding, there are never enough or the right words except those spoken by Jesus, "For God so loved the world that He gave His only begotten Son"...for me (John 3:16).

As we conclude, Saul recognizes he now has a *new allegiance* and a *new assignment*, when he asks, "[L]ord what will thou have me to do?" (Acts 9:6). Interestingly Jesus says go and wait (Acts 9:6). Furthermore, where you were once leading the way, you will now be led (Acts 9:8). The spiritually critical result of this encounter with Jesus will be Saul's loathing of God's people will be replaced with love for them. He will go from being the persecutor to being the persecuted (Acts 9:23). From a spectator watching the people of God he will now be a participator doing the things of God. Where he once breathed threatening and slaughtering (Acts 9:1) he will now be preaching to the lost and praying for the saved. His passion for stoning believers will be replaced by a passion to strengthen them. Keeping people from the teachings of Christ will give way to bringing people to a saving knowledge of Him. Once where he ridiculed these who believed, he will now rejoice, as does heaven over one sinner that repenteth (Luke 15:7). Saul the one time puppet master will become Paul a pulpit messenger.

As it did with Saul, ladies and gentlemen, all that Saul went from and ultimately became should be our testimony as well. All that happened in Saul's life and all that has happened in my life as well, was in response to the question Jesus asked Saul, and the same one He once asked me, "Steve, Steve, why persecutest thou me"?

Chapter Outline

I. Saul's Contempt for the Church
   A. Saul's Unique Qualifications
      1. His Parturition
      2. His Education
      3. His Premeditation
      4. His Conviction

II. Saul's Charge Against the Church
   A. Attempting to Suppress the message of the church
   B. Attempting to Silence the members of the church

III. Saul's Conversation with the Lord
   A. The Light He Saw
   B. The Lord Who Spoke
      1. The Accusation Saul must answer
      2. The Answer Saul requests
      3. The Acknowledgement Jesus confirms

IV. Saul's Conversion
   A. Saul's Response
      1. He was trembling
      2. It was astonishing
   B. He has a New Allegiance
   C. He has a New Assignment

Chapter 7
"But who say ye that I am?"
Personal Opinion
Matthew 16:15-18

As I alluded to in the first chapter, Jesus now asks the question that, depending on one's answer, will determine a person's eternity. We now move to the focus of the verses in Matthew 16:15, where, He (Jesus) saith unto them, "But who say ye that I am?" So from public opinion we discussed in Chapter 1, the emphasis is now on the most important question a person will ever answer, which is what one's Personal Opinion of who Jesus is. Peter's answer to the question is as profound as it is prophetic as he declares, "Thou art the Christ, the Son of the living God" (Matthew 16:16).

First, his answer goes beyond *enlightenment or education*. Did you notice what Jesus says in response…"for flesh and blood hath not revealed it unto thee" (verse 17). Enlightenment and education are flesh and blood responses. As an aside, it is getting to be a challenge to distinguish between them, as the world has confused and confounded the two merging concepts when they should not do so.

It is amazing the amount of information that is available through the use of technology. Literally, millions of facts and figures are at our fingertips. Access to the Internet has expounded exponentially how much, and in a matter of hundredths of a second how many pages upon pages of sources on specifics pertaining to a topic becomes instantaneously available. Not only is information accessible for personal use but also universities and colleges have degree programs that utilize on-line delivery services so people can have the benefit of obtaining degrees from the comfort of their own home. Having access to information does not translate to being enlightened so it is not an issue of having access. Nor does being able to obtain information necessarily equate to correct application as it pertains to the spiritual, as Jesus so stated in His answer to Peter.

For centuries, the educated have attempted to dismiss Jesus. It amazes me how the public will embrace secular education and secular views regarding religion but will dismiss religious education pertaining to the things of God. You have heard the argument of the educationally arrogant as they question how one could believe in a God that… would let a baby go to hell, would create a place called hell (for that matter) would not condone the gay/lesbian/homosexual lifestyle, does not stop world hunger, or the God they know loves everyone (which He does, but hopefully you know what I mean by this) no matter the depths of their depravity…and the list goes on and on. In fact, you can probably add your own examples from your personal experiences when you have heard the educationally elite attempt to explain away or reject who Jesus is based on understanding rooted in the confines of human flesh and blood.

Among the educated, as mentioned in the first chapter, Evolution and the Big Bang Theory are heralded while Creationism and Intelligent Design is summarily dismissed, all in the light of enlightenment and education. In fact as this was being written a "celebrity" on a popular nationally syndicated talk show had the audacity to say it was child abuse to not teach a child evolution! Can you hear the underpinning arrogance of such a statement? Somewhere in the name of education or enlightenment we are now being told to accept ungodly ideology. Whether these concepts about Jesus originated in the classroom or is ultimately determined in the courtroom, reasoning based on man's intellectualism has and will continue to attempt to make Jesus less than who He has been and will forever be, the Son of the living God. So the flesh and blood of enlightenment and education is not the basis on which to answer the personal question of who Jesus is.

As was the case in Chapter 1 where I applied "isms" to the context of Popular Opinion, I am now going to expand the concept of isms and apply them to enlightenment and education in the context of Personal Opinion. The first as related to what a person's opinion of Jesus would be is exemplified by agnosticism-not knowing if there is/is not a god. Basically, this person has no opinion or attempts to be neutral as to God. Biblically, this is recognized and refuted in Romans 1:20-21. Verse 20 unequivocally says "[F]or the invisible things of him from the creation of the world are clearly seen, being understood by the things that are made, even his eternal power and Godhead, so that they are without excuse."

Now, you may be remembering the discussions of the *"isms"* in the first chapter and those "universally" seeing a god in the universe, nature, plants, et cetera; yet there is a difference in seeing "a," or god in these "isms" as opposed to seeing "the" God of Genesis 1:1. So, no matter how enlightened or educated one may be and thus call themselves *agnostics*. Chapter 1 verse 21 of Romans puts the responsibility on the individual as, "when they knew God, they glorified him not as God...became vain in their imaginations and their foolish heart was darkened."

Following closely behind and in many ways comparable is *atheism*-the denial of the existence of God. Obviously, the verses of Romans 1 used above would be applicable and relevant to an analysis of atheism. However, I want to take a bit of a different tack but still remain true to the spirit and letter of God's truth. Adding to the definition describing an atheist as one denying the existence of God, I want to add the atheist saying there is no God "for me."

Dr. Jerry Vines, former pastor at First Baptist Church in Jacksonville, FL introduced this to me with his commentary on Psalms 14:1 where it begins by saying, "[T]he fool hath said in his heart, There is no God." Through his study of the Hebrew words, Dr. Vines concluded the interpretation and thus the application of this verse lent itself to the concept the psalmist was conveying was the fool says-there is no god "for me."

As I now expound on this, a New Testament example would be that in Acts 26. Here we see Paul defending himself and at the same time witnessing to Herod Agrippa. In verse 28, we see his response to Paul's pleading by announcing, "Almost thou persuades me to be a Christian." So, much like Psalms 14, Agrippa declares, as does atheism, there is no god "for me."

Enlightenment and Education also can be seen in *humanism*-man is his own god. In the Humanist Manifesto II, the last sentence of the first religious section specifically says, "no deity will save us; we must save ourselves." This obviously contradicts Biblical declarations pronouncing...for all have sinned (Romans 3:23), the wages of sin is death (Romans 6:23), if we confess our sins (1 John 1:9), and what must I do to be saved-believe...Believe on the Lord Jesus Christ (Acts 16:30-31). We add to that, the familiar, faithful teachings of Ephesians 2:8-9. It is interesting to note, the Manifesto uses the word "save" as related to a deity and themselves. The question would then be, in what context are they using the word? Questioning, without speculating, what is the humanist saying they must "save" themselves "from" or "to" for that matter?

We see this all about me attitude flaunted at every opportunity. We have what I have termed *"meism"* commonly portrayed in spirit and song, "what have you done for 'me' lately," as well as the phrase, "it is all about 'me.'" My Space, Facebook, LinkedIn are examples of where society has encouraged self-promotion. Interestingly, we get offended when someone violates our personal space, but will encourage them to visit our public space.

Understand, I realize these are not necessarily evil or vile in and of themselves, but are used as examples of ways we have extended the notion of me first, God later, or never. As concerning social media, that context is expanded as a picture taken of one's self is called a selfie. I am now going to ramp that up one additional level, by creating another new term-selfme.

Having said that, I am not saying all photographs of this nature are self-absorbing, just that we have taken it to a humanistic level, where again, it is all about the person and their self-assurance, reliance, and edification. Essentially, notwithstanding other things the humanist may believe, their personal opinion about God, in its most simple form is-I am my god.

Linguistically, as described above, we even have developed isms to define our beliefs related to God. Some of these declare we can substitute God's righteousness with our standard of goodness as dictated by our perception of the universe, science, morality, fairness, compassion, philanthropy, or fair play. The result of these isms are an attempt to reach up to pull God down to our level as opposed to lifting up outstretched arms to be lifted by God to heights we can only access by His grace.

Peter's answer also goes beyond the enlightenment of *pathos*. The Greek philosopher, Aristotle felt to reach an audience the subject matter had to appeal to one's *logos, ethos*, or pathos. Logos was based on reasoning, or what we might compare to making a logical argument. Ethos dealt with convincing a person based on the writer or speaker's credibility.

Pathos was the method used to appeal to one's emotions. Seeing Jesus for who He is goes beyond the emotions; however, to make sure this is clear from the outset, our relationship with Jesus is emotional. In my life I have cried, laughed, pleaded, praised, argued, been comforted by and complained to Jesus, all of which are emotional experiences. Yet, no matter the highs or lows emotionally our relationship with Christ is not based on emotions.

In the Chapter "What seek Ye?' I related the emotions my wife and I might experience or express in the marriage relationship; yet, no matter how we "felt" we were still married. I then went on to say there are times in our relationship with Christ when our emotions cannot be trusted. Here is another example of how, no matter how I feel, Jesus still loves me, no matter my emotions.

There have been times when I have done something spiritual, so to speak, (like writing a book) and am emotionally fulfilled, resulting in positive emotions as I may emotionally felt I have curried favor with God. At this point I am on an emotional high, experiencing all God has called me to be and I have been faithful to that call.

Then, from literally nowhere, I think, say, or do something sinful and my emotions change. I truly ask God's forgiveness and He is faithful to forgive me. Yet incredibly, I may repeat the same sin. Emotionally, I feel bad, really bad, and am broken hearted, wondering how God can continue to love and forgive me. My emotions have gone from elation to depression. Yet, although I am emotionally distraught, God says, "as far as the east is from the west, "so far hath he removed our transgressions from us" (Psalms 103:12). The result is no matter how good or bad I have felt, God loved me no more, no less based on my emotions. He just Loves Me. You may have heard, a faith that cannot be tested cannot be trusted. Praise God, that is not applicable to emotions.

This emotional argument goes right to what Jesus said in verse 17 of Matthew 16... "for flesh and blood hath not revealed it unto thee, but my Father, who is in heaven." Referring back to the Four Spiritual Laws we discussed previously, it has a train with three cars attached to it representing, in order, fact, faith and feeling. Peter had witnessed the fact that Jesus was who He said He was, had put his faith there and it would not change, no matter his, or, in the present day, our feelings.

Peter's answer surpasses the boundaries of religion as well. Based on the words I used to find world religions, a Google search revealed there are twenty-two "major" religions. Using approximate numbers, Christianity is listed at the top with 2.1 billion and in the twenty second spot is Scientology with 500 thousand adherents. To be clear, I am not going to attempt to define, classify or clarify what is meant by religion, but only reporting my search results. To cloud the issue even further would be to add the number of religious denominations to the argument. Suffice it to say, man has attempted to explain his existence and has done, and continues to do so, through religion. Throughout the ages, man has attempted to define the boundaries of religious belief. We have done so by, at its lowest common denominator, lowering or eliminating God's standards of righteousness and holiness.

As related to the self-edifying and self-promoting isms of the world as interconnected with religions, Peter's answer to Jesus' question goes beyond them as well. Now we have the inclusion of *illuminism*-belief in an inward spiritual light, *latitudinarianism*-doctrine of broad liberality in religious belief and conduct, *omnism*-belief in all religions and *psilanthropism*-denial of Christ's divinity.[3] The result is each in its own blasphemous way has become a religion. From acknowledging or not acknowledging a supreme being, to edifying ourselves, or finally, to believing in no one or anything, all religions attempt to create a mechanism to worship someone other or something other than the true God of 1 John 5:20. This verse says, incontrovertibly, "that we may know him that is true; and we are in him that is true, even in his Son Jesus Christ. This is the true God, and eternal life."

This religious, philosophical approach was nothing new as Jesus dealt with all these in His day. From disbelief in His deity (Pharisees), to disbelief of the resurrection (Sadducees), to affirmation of man in view of the world (Herodians), Jesus met the challenge raised by religion. Additionally, the scriptures had to deal with its isms as well. One was *Gnosticism*. Much like its fraternal twin, Epicureanism, Gnosticism believed things done in the body did not affect the spirit as they were totally separated. The result was anything, no matter how

---

[3] For a list and definition of a host of isms see: The Phrontistery, n a thinking-place [Gr phrontisterion from phrontistes a thinker, from phroneein to think]. Located at http://phrontistery.info/isms.html.

sinful done in the body, had no effect on the spirit. In modern day jargon the concept would be "it it feels good do it," or "just do it," in the case of a national advertising campaign for a major sports retailer. I might add, we have taken that concept to a different level as we not only do "it," whatever "it" is, but we let the world watch. It is amazing to me the number of reality shows that exploit sin.

Actually, there are two types of participants- those who do and those who watch. We have taken voyeurism to a new level, as we cannot wait to tune into the next episode of cheating, lying, stealing, or infidelity. From housewives to bachelors/ bachelorettes, we welcome and watch people exploit their sin, while starving their soul. The psalmist in Psalm 106:15 recognized this when commenting on the children of Israel's lustfulness in the wilderness when he said, "[A]nd he (God) gave them their request but sent leanness into their soul." Even in the editing process of this book another "reality show," Dating Naked has been introduced to the airways. The church uses God's grace to justify its sin. The implication is one can sin carte blanche, and then run to God. Indulge the body, ignore the soul, justified by calling it a religion has been a theme throughout the ages.

Tragically, this thinking has infiltrated the church or at least those who profess to be Christians. Not too long ago a poll was taken asking Christians when they would consider having sex in the context of a dating relationship. Astonishingly, 61% said they would have casual sex without being in love. In the same survey, only 11% said they would abstain from having sex until they were married.[4] Ladies and gentlemen this is a travesty and the height of hypocrisy. This is what religion espouses, not what a relationship with Jesus entails. Paul knew it was not religion, as defined by man and ultimately exemplified by his and this generation's rationale of their sin that prompted his response, and Jesus was about to verify that very fact.

So if it was not enlightenment, education, or religion that prompted Peter's declaration then what was it? Jesus answers this for us by saying, …"but my Father, who is in heaven" (Matthew 16:17). Those of us who have grown up in church have had it reiterated over and over again, that the difference between Christianity and religion is a personal relationship with Christ. This relationship with Jesus begins with a divine revelation. I do not want to make this a mystical or lighting bolt type of experience, nor do I want to downplay the reality of God working in this manner, but I do want to show what I believe brought Peter to this point.

First, Peter has seen *Jesus the man*. John 1:41-42 is the text documenting Peter's first encounter with Jesus. In one meeting, Peter's life is changed and ultimately, as I will discuss later his name will be changed. Over the next three years Peter will be Jesus' constant, close companion. He will see Jesus deal lovingly with innocent young children and harshly with older adults. He will witness those

---

[4] Morgan Lee, Christian Dating Culture: Majority of Christian Singles Reject Idea of Waiting Until Marriage to Have Sex. The Christian Post, February 14, 2014. Accessed at http://exministries.tv/christian-mingle-survey-61-of-christians-singles-are-willing-to-have-casual-sex/.

undocumented things Jesus would have naturally done like laughing, working, playing, singing, and sleeping. Unlike you and I, as we fight to restrain our human nature when faced with the circumstances of life, that was never the case with Jesus. He never reacted in a manner that would have betrayed His character. No off colored jokes to entertain, no foul language if He stubbed his toe, Peter saw Jesus the man. Peter saw Jesus be Jesus all the time.

Peter also saw *Jesus do the miraculous* as related to him personally. Without recounting the numerous miracles depicted in the scriptures, the emphasis here relates to those of which Peter was specifically the subject. The first would be his call to salvation and service as depicted in John 1:35-42 and Matthew 4:18-20.

Just to be clear, salvation no matter how sensational the circumstances may or may not be, salvation is a miracle of God. For a person to see themselves as sinners, understand Christ died for them and then accept His death for the payment for their sins and accept Him as Lord and Savior is in every sense of the word, a miracle. We next look on Peter's witnessing Jesus healing those who are sick. Early in Jesus' ministry, as recorded in Matthew 8:14, He, Jesus, sees Peter's wife's mother who is sick of a fever. In verse 15...he touched her hand and the fever left her; and she arose and ministered unto him. As such, Peter saw *Jesus do the miraculous* as linked to his personal life and his family.

The next of emphasis, although certainly not the last, of which Peter was and would be the benefactor, are his walking on the water and ministering for the Master. For the first, we again go to the book of

Matthew, Chapter 15.[5] As you recall, Jesus had sent the disciples out in a boat so He could deal with the multitudes, verses 22-23. Ultimately, there was a storm and in the midst, Jesus walking on the sea approaches the boat (verses 24-27). The disciples, thinking He is a ghost cry out, Jesus answers, and Peter wanting confirmation it is Jesus says..."Lord if it be thou, bid me come unto thee on the water" (verse 28). Peter comes out, verse 29, and ultimately cries out, verse 30 and Jesus catches...verse 31...And immediately Jesus stretched forth his hand, and caught him.

As miraculous as was Peter's salvation and seeing Jesus work in his life, the circumstances of his service are equally compelling. In each of the four gospels there are the accounts of Peter's actions/inactions associated with his denials during the arrest and trial of Jesus.[6] Recall the discussion herein related to feelings and our relationship to Jesus? Peter's feelings let him down, but the facts and his faith did not as we shall soon see. Admittedly, the denials would be after Peter's revelation concerning who Jesus is, but it is important as related to Peter's name change which Jesus states in Matthew 16:18 as to his impact on spreading the gospel.

---

[5] Should you be interested, here is an outline related to Peter's walking on the water experience: Peter's Desire, He comes out, 15:28-29; Peter's Defeat, He cries out, 15:30; and Peter's Deliverance, Jesus catches/pulls him out, 15:10-31.

[6] These can be summed up as Peter Declares His Allegiance, Denounces His Associations, and Denies His Association. However, something that is overlooked is the other Disciple's Agreement, see Matthew 26:35, Peter said unto him, Though I should die with thee, yet will I not deny thee. Likewise also said all the disciples (emphasis added).

Names and what they are associated with are very telling. In today's society businesses entities and people are known by one name. People recognize the names Nike, Coke, Apple as well as Elvis, Oprah, and Tiger. Jesus in Matthew 16:18 now acknowledges the one word meaning of Peter's name-*petros, a pebble* while contrasting that with the statement Peter previously made. Unlike some who place great prominence on the petros of Peter's stature on which to build the church, the importance is not on the pebble but on the *Petra*-the massive rock of Peter's statement in verse 16, "[T]hou art the Christ, the Son of the living God." Paul, when reminding the Corinthians of what God did for the Israelites while in the wilderness in 1 Corinthians 10:1-5, specifically in verse 4 it says, [A]nd did all drink the same spiritual drink: for they drank of that spiritual Rock that followed them: and that Rock was Christ. There we see, as He was to the Israelites, Christ is the Rock of my sustenance. In Psalms 62:6 Christ is the Rock of my salvation and in Isaiah 28:16 and reiterated in 1 Peter 2:1-8 Christ is the Rock of the structure of my life, on which my life is built and stands.

We have looked at the Petros and Petra as related to the church, but lastly let's look at the *possession of the church*. Note the wording of Matthew 16:18 as Jesus says, "I will build "my" church. Some churches are known for having *great pastors, great programs, and being beautiful places*, which they should as God is worthy of the very best. However, as they are great pillars on which to build, the most precious treasure within the church is its people. Jesus built His church on the *people who are blood washed, born again*. It is the people who are the testimony to the life changing power of Jesus. People can, and will, argue spiritual and doctrinal issues with you and I. They will say the church is hypocritical and has in the past harbored heresies and heretics. In essence all that may be true, but the world cannot argue with a changed life and Jesus changes lives. He changed mine and has given me the *privilege to proclaim* the gospel (Matthew 28:20) all the while promising to *protect and preserve* me in the process (2 Tim. 4:18).

Being the Christ, the Son of the living God, Jesus lived, died and rose again for those who acknowledge their sin, accept Him as Lord and Savior and as such have answered eternally the most important question anyone can be asked-"But who say ye that I am?"

Chapter Outline

I. Education-cannot make one smart enough

II. Enlightenment-cannot make one self-aware enough
    A. Pathos
    B. Logos
    C. Ethos
    D. The isms
        1. Agnosticism-not knowing if there is/is not a God
        2. Atheism-there is no God for Me
        3. Humanism-man is his own god
            a. Meism-it is all about Me

III. Religion-cannot make one spiritual enough
    A. The isms of Jesus' day
        1. Gnosticism-the body and spirit are totally separate
            a. Epicureanism-pleasure is the sole good
        2. Illuminism-belief in an inward spiritual light
        3. Latitudinarianism-doctrine of broad liberality in religious belief and conduct
        4. Omnism-belief in all religions
        5. Psilanthropism-denial of Christ's divinity

IV. Peter and What he saw that lead to his statement
    A. He saw Jesus the Man
    B. He saw Jesus and His Miracles
    C. He saw Jesus Ministering

V. Peter-Petros, a pebble

VI. Christ-Petra, a stone
    A. His Possession of the church
        1. Great Pastors
        2. Great Programs
        3. Beautiful Places
        4. Born Again People
            a. My Privilege to Proclaim
            b. Jesus's Promise to Protect and Preserve

ENDNOTES

As I did in my first book, it would be remiss for me not to share the circumstances leading to my accepting Christ as my personal savior. Salvation is a miracle and I experienced such a miracle. You have probably heard testimonies of those Christ saved from a life of alcohol or drug abuse. Or maybe you know someone who was on the brink of fiscal collapse or was the victim or instigator of a dysfunctional personal relationship that resulted in his or her coming to Christ.

My testimony is none of the above. In fact, I believe it to be more compelling, as by all accounts, I did not need a savior. As a child, for the most part, I was obedient and compliant. Through my younger and mid teen years during the 60s and 70s I did not consume alcohol, take illicit and mind altering drugs, nor was I sexually active, which for that time period made me a bit abnormal. Actually, my attitude was counter cultural as I did not "do it" since "everyone was doing it," a popular theme of the times. So, in that regard I was a bit of a rebel. Bottom line, a person who has experienced the fruit of their sin understands their need to change their lives, but that was not my plight.

In high school, athletics makes for popularity and prestige. As an athlete I had both and one of those perks lead to me being elected vice-president of our high school's chapter of the Fellowship of Christian Athletes (FCA). I had attended meetings, but even now cannot remember what was discussed; except for one where I played and contrasted the words of a popular song of the times to the greatness of God. Hopefully, it did not damage the cause of Christ. As my family never attended church, God was more conceptual than personal. I understood right from wrong and figured if one picked right that was God's side and if I picked wrong, it was the devil's side. Evaluating my spiritual life at the time, I was looking pretty good.

As a FCA officer, I was given the opportunity to attend its camp in Rome, Georgia. The week long camp revolved around morning teaching sessions, athletic competition and then nightly assemblies lead by famous professional and college athletes, all spiritually based. A minister-humorist, Grady Nutt conducted all the morning sessions. He used his book, Being Me-Self, You Bug Me which revolved around the statement, "I am a person of worth, created in the image of God, to relate and to live" as the theme for each session. Using that statement and his wit and practicality he brought me to the realization that God, through the revelation of His Son Jesus Christ, was more than a spiritual concept and that I could be involved with Him in a personal relationship. As a result of his teachings, by my bedside after a night session, I asked Jesus to forgive me of my sin and to be my Lord and Savior. Without realizing it, I had gone from convicted sinner to converted saint.

Returning home, I went a new, yet baby Christian. As mentioned previously, my family did not go to church and unfortunately I remained in an infant state spiritually. My family neither condoned nor condemned my newfound Christianity, but did not do anything to facilitate it. I knew if I were to die my destination was heaven, but there was still the here and now I needed to deal with. It was not until my graduation from high school and my first car that I began a spiritual growth spurt. With my new transportation I was able to drive myself to church. In fact, when a young lady asked me to go to church with her my response was that I knew all about that "stuff." At that point I really did not know what I did not know. I also made a public profession of my faith in that church when I followed the Lord in Believers' Baptism.

By God's grace and the miracle of my salvation in that summer of 1971 He has continued to teach me. Some lessons I learned faster, others slower but my spiritual education has continued. However, I can and do say with all conviction I took learning the Word and Ways of God very seriously. I knew it was my responsibility to take advantage of solid Biblical doctrine and to know in whom and what I believed. God has graciously allowed me to share what He has taught me to others along the way, which is probably why He taught it to me. This book is an outgrowth of the Grace He has shown me and if He so wills, others will share in His Amazing Grace, grow, and share it with others. My hope is that we will, as Jesus did with those with whom He had contact, follow His example and ask the right questions. May this book help facilitate and be a blessing in that process.

Scripture Index

By Chapter and Page Number

Chapter 1
"Who do men say that I, the Son of man, am?"

Genesis	2:18	page 8
Genesis	3:19	page 8
1 Kings	16:30	page 3
1 Kings	16:33	page 3
1 Kings	17	page 3
1 Kings	17:12-16	page 5
1 Kings	17:17	page 6
1 Kings	18:13	page 4
1 Kings	21	page 4
Psalms	56:3	page 10
Jeremiah	2:2	page 12
Jeremiah	2:11	page 11, 12
Jeremiah	2:12	page 12
Jeremiah	2:13	page 11, 12
Jeremiah	39	page 11
Jeremiah	52	page 11
Matthew	2:2	page 13
Matthew	2:16	page 13
Matthew	3:11	page 2
Matthew	3:14	page 2
Matthew	8:6	page 6
Matthew	14:1-12	page 2
Matthew	16: 13-14	page 2
Matthew	21:11	page 11
Matthew	24	page 12

Mark	5:39-40	page 6
Mark	5:22-43	page 6
Mark	15:33	page 13
Luke	1:13	page 2
Luke	1:16	page 2
Luke	1:17	page 2
Luke	1:18	page 2
Luke	1:24	page 2
Luke	1:36	page 2
Luke	1:41	page 2
Luke	3:3-20	page 2
Luke	10:40-42	page 7
Luke	7:11-18	page 7
Luke	11:13	page 10
Luke	13:34-35	page 13
Luke	19:41-44	page 13
Luke	21:20-24	page 12
John	19:15	page 5, 11, 12
John	11	page 7
John	11:21	page 8
John	11:33	page 10
John	11:35	page 10
Hebrews	9:27	page 9
Revelation	5:4	page 10

Chapter 2
"Why Are Ye So Fearful. How is It That Ye Have No Faith"

Exodus	14:16	page 28
Exodus	17:10-13	page 28
Zechariah	3:2	page 25

Malachi	3:11	page 25
Matthew	4:18	page 21
Matthew	4:19	page 21
Matthew	17:15	page 25
Mark	4:1-12	page 17
Mark	4:13-20	page 17
Mark	4:21-25	page 18
Mark	4:26-29	page 18
Mark	4:30-34	page 18
Mark	4:9	page 17
Mark	4:35-41	page 17
Mark	3:36	page 20
Mark	4:36	page 20
Mark	4:37	page 18, 20
Mark	4:38	page 21
Mark	4:39	page 25, 26
Mark	4:40	page 26
Mark	4:41	page 27
Mark	8:32-33	page 25
Mark	14	page 25
John	21:1-11	page 21
Ephesians	2:2	page 25
Hebrews	13:5	page 24

Chapter 3
"What wilt thou that I should do unto thee?"

Genesis	13:10	page 40
Joshua	6:20	page 32
2 Kings	6:5-6	page 33
Proverbs	95:7-8	page 36

Matthew	1	page 35
Matthew	6:8	page 39
Matthew	14:21	page 35
Matthew	20:29	page 31
Matthew	20:30	page 32
Mark	3:1-6	page 35
Mark	5:28	page 37
Mark	10:46-52	page 31
Mark	10:47	page 34
Mark	10:48	page 35, 37
Mark	10:49	page 37
Mark	10:51	page 38
Mark	10:52	page 42
Luke	18:35	page 32
Luke	7:47	page 35
Acts	22:8	page 34
1 Corinthians	6:19	page 42
Hebrews	3:7-8	page 37
Hebrews	3:15	page 37
James	1:22-23	page 39

Chapter 4
"Why callest thou me good?"

Genesis	3:5	page 58
Exodus	20:3	page 50
Exodus	20:4	page 50
Exodus	20:17	page 51
Exodus	32:1	page 50
Exodus	32:1-6	page 50
1 Samuel	16:7	page 54
Psalms	86:5	page 56
Psalms	119:68	page 56
Proverbs	4:3	page 50

Matthew	5:8	page 49
Matthew	5:17	page 49
Matthew	7:21-22	page 49
Matthew	19	page 45
Mark	10	page 45
Luke	9:23	page 53
Luke	12:11-21	page 51
Luke	12:19	page 51
Luke	18:18-30	page 45
Luke	18:18	page 46, 51, 56
Luke	18:19	page 55
Luke	18:20	page 49
Luke	18:21	page 48
Luke	18:22	page 50, 52
Luke	18:23	page 51, 52
Luke	18:24	page 51
Luke	18:24-25	page 52, 53
Luke	18:26	page 53
Luke	18:27	page 54
Luke	18:28	page 54
Luke	18:29-30	page 55
Luke	19-26	page 51
Luke	20:24	page 51
John	10:10	page 55
1 Corinthians	1:9	page 55
Hebrews	2:2	page 54

Chapter 5
"What seek ye?"

Genesis	3:21	page 63
Exodus	20:4	page 66
Psalms	51:10	page 64
Isaiah	53:7	page 63

Isaiah	64:4	page 70
Matthew	3:17	page 62
Matthew	9:9-10	page 71
Matthew	27:57-61	page 71
Luke	9:58	page 72
Luke	18:18-27	page 66
Luke	18:21	page 66
Luke	18:22	page 66
Luke	18:23	page 66
John	1:35-42	page 61
John	1:15-19	page 61
John	1:20-26	page 61
John	1:27-54	page 61
John	1:37	page 64
John	1:38	page 71, 73
John	1:39	page 72
John	1:40	page 73
John	1:41	page 73
John	3	page 62, 69
John	3:34	page 62
John	5:29	page 62
John	5:35-36	page 62
John	6:30-59	page 66
John	6:60	page 66
John	6:67	page 67
John	12:1	page 71
John	14:1-6	page 70
Mark	4:1-12	page 67
Mark	4:13-20	page 67
Mark	4:16	page 67
Mark	4:17	page 67
Mark	14:14	page 71
Mark	6:29	page 62
Acts	8:32	page 63

Romans	3:23	page 64
Romans	3:25	page 64
1 Corinthians	2:9	page 70
Ephesians	1:3	page 69
Hebrews	9:22	page 63
Hebrews	9:28	page 63
1 Peter	1:9	page 64

Chapter 6
"Saul, Saul, why persecutest thou me?"

Exodus	3:12	page 83
Deuteronomy	21:23	page 78
Psalms	107:12	page 86
Proverbs	1:7	page 87
Proverbs	9:10	page 87
Proverbs	15:33	page 87
Matthew	2:2	page 82
Matthew	7:13-14	page 81
Mark	14:61-62	page 78
Mark	14:64	page 78
Luke	15:7	page 88
John	2:20	page 78
John	3:16	page 88
John	8:12	page 82
John	14:6	page 81
John	18:13	page 79
John	18:14	page 79
John	18:24	page 79
Acts	5:34	page 77
Acts	5:35	page 78
Acts	7:54-8:1	page 81
Acts	8:1	page 77
Acts	9:1	page 79, 82, 88

Acts	9:1-6	page 75
Acts	9:2	page 79, 81
Acts	9:3	page 81
Acts	9:4	page 82
Acts	9:5	page 82, 83
Acts	9:6	page 85, 88
Acts	9:8	page 88
Acts	9:13	page 82
Acts	9:15	page 75
Acts	9:23	page 88
Acts	11:26	page 78
Acts	13:9	page 75, 82
Acts	19:9	page 81
Acts	19:23	page 81
Acts	22:3	page 76, 77
Acts	22:4	page 77, 81
Acts	22:6	page 82
Acts	24:14	page 81
Acts	24:22	page 81
Acts	26:11	page 85
Romans	3:23	page 80
Romans	6:23	page 80
Romans	12:19	page 82
Ephesians	5:25	page 76
Ephesians	5:26	page 76
Ephesians	5:27	page 76
Ephesians	5:29	page 76
Philippians	3:5	page 76, 77
2 Peter	1:16-19	page 82
Revelation	3:2	page 85
Revelation	22:16	page 82

Chapter 7
"But Who Say Ye That I Am?"

Genesis	1	page 94
Psalms	14	page 95
Psalms	14:1	page 94
Psalms	62:6	page 104
Isaiah	28:16	page 104
Matthew	4:18-20	page 102
Matthew	8:14	page 102
Matthew	8:15	page 101
Matthew	15:10-31	page 102
Matthew	15:22-23	page 102
Matthew	15:24-27	page 102
Matthew	15:28	page 102
Matthew	15:29	page 102
Matthew	16:15	page 91
Matthew	16:16	page 91, 103
Matthew	16:17	page 91, 98, 101
Matthew	16:18	page 103
Matthew	26:35	page 103
Matthew	28:20	page 105
John	1:35-42	page 102
John	1:41-42	page 101
Acts	16:30-31	page 95
Acts	26	page 95
Romans	1	page 94
Romans	1:20	page 93
Romans	1:21	page 93, 94
Romans	3:23	page 95
Romans	6:23	page 95
1 Corinthians	10:1-5	page 104
Ephesians	2:8-9	page 95
2 Timothy	4:8	page 104

1 Peter	2:1-8	page 104
1 John	1:9	page 95
1 John	5:20	page 99

These Things We Believe

We hope you have enjoyed Steve Dedmon's work, *Questions Jesus Asked*. Have you had the opportunity to read his other title, his first book, *These Things We Believe*? Both books are available through BluewaterPress LLC at www.bluewaterpress.com and through www.amazon.com and other online retailers. Please contact BluewaterPress LLC for bulk ordering discount pricing for both of Mr. Dedmon's books.

www.ingramcontent.com/pod-product-compliance
Lightning Source LLC
LaVergne TN
LVHW011355080426
835511LV00005B/301